HOUSE OF LORDS

Science and Technology Committee

6th Report of Session 2005–06

Ageing: Scientific Aspects

Follow-up

Report with Evidence

Ordered to be printed 14 March and published 22 March 2006

Published by the Authority of the House of Lords

London : The Stationery Office Limited
£11.00

HL Paper 146

Science and Technology Committee

The Science and Technology Committee is appointed by the House of Lords in each session "to consider science and technology".

Current Membership

The Members of the Science and Technology Committee are:

> Lord Broers (Chairman)
> Baroness Finlay of Llandaff
> Lord Howie of Troon
> Lord Mitchell
> Lord Patel
> Lord Paul
> Baroness Perry of Southwark
> Baroness Platt of Writtle
> Earl of Selborne
> Baroness Sharp of Guildford
> Lord Sutherland of Houndwood
> Lord Taverne
> Lord Winston
> Lord Young of Graffham

For membership and declared interests of the Sub-Committee which conducted the original inquiry, see the Committee's 1st Report of session 2005–06, *Ageing: Scientific Aspects* (HL Paper 20-I).

Information about the Committee and Publications

Information about the Science and Technology Committee, including details of current inquiries, can be found on the internet at http://www.parliament.uk/hlscience/. Committee publications, including reports, press notices, transcripts of evidence and government responses to reports, can be found at the same address.

Committee reports are published by The Stationery Office by Order of the House.

General Information

General information about the House of Lords and its Committees, including guidance to witnesses, details of current inquiries and forthcoming meetings is on the internet at: http://www.parliament.uk/about_lords/about_lords.cfm.

Contacts for the Science and Technology Committee

All correspondence should be addressed to:
The Clerk of the Science and Technology Committee
Committee Office
House of Lords
London
SW1A 0PW

The telephone number for general enquiries is 020 7219 6075.
The Committee's email address is hlscience@parliament.uk.

CONTENTS

Ageing: Scientific Aspects Follow-up

THE COMMITTEE'S COMMENTARY ON THE GOVERNMENT RESPONSE

1. In June 2004 we appointed a Sub-Committee to examine the Scientific Aspects of Ageing. Our special interest was in the biological aspects of the ageing process, and in those areas of research which might particularly benefit older people, and delay the onset of life-threatening conditions, long-term illnesses and disabilities. We examined whether there was sufficient research capability in the United Kingdom, whether the correct research priorities had been identified, and how effectively research was co-ordinated.

2. Our Report was published on 21 July 2005.[1] Although the Government had only just agreed to reduce the time allowed for the preparation of responses to our reports from six to two months, various extensions and delays meant that we did not receive a response until 4 November. The response is reprinted as written evidence.

3. The matters covered by the Report are the responsibility of a number of departments, most prominent among them the Department of Trade and Industry (DTI) (of which the Office of Science and Technology (OST) is part) and the Department of Health (DoH). It is of course for the Government to assign responsibility for preparing responses. We were nevertheless a little surprised to learn that in this case the response was co-ordinated by the Department for Work and Pensions (DWP), a department which had declined to submit written evidence to us.[2] The response was signed by Stephen Timms MP, the Minister of State for Pensions Reform, even though pensions were expressly outside the remit of our inquiry.[3] We appreciate that the Secretary of State for Work and Pensions bears the title of "Government champion of older people", but neither the minister nor his department has a significant responsibility for the scientific aspects of ageing.

4. The response is lengthy and detailed—and, in our view, deeply disappointing. We therefore took the unusual step of sending it to some of our original witnesses, and to Professor Tom Kirkwood (who acted as Specialist Adviser to our original inquiry), to seek their views. We are grateful to those who replied, and their replies are printed as written evidence.[4] It will be seen that, without exception, they share our disappointment, expressing it in sometimes forceful language.

5. This disappointment does not stem primarily from the fact that our recommendations have almost without exception been rejected. It stems from the fact that, if the response is to be taken at face value, older people,

---

[1] First Report, Session 2005–06, HL Paper 20.

[2] First Report, paragraph 7.18.

[3] See the Call for Evidence published as Appendix 3 to our First Report.

[4] We also received a reply from Professor Cyrus Cooper, Director and Professor of Rheumatology, MRC Epidemiology Resource Centre, which we have not treated as evidence.

their families, those who care for them, those responsible for their health, and ultimately all of us, will suffer from the Government's failure to acknowledge the problems and opportunities presented by an ageing society.

6.   It is particularly disappointing that the Government seem to wish to "pigeon-hole" ageing research, as if ageing were an isolated, discrete problem, and that research into ageing must necessarily compete with research into other areas. Thus the response reproduces the familiar mantra that "given finite resources, there will always be a need to balance competing priorities for research". As we sought to demonstrate in our Report—a point repeated by Professor Kirkwood in his written comments—ageing is a continuum, affecting all of us all the time. He also reiterates the point made in our Report, that generic research into the process of ageing, far from being in competition with research into specific conditions affecting older people, may be "the most direct route to developing novel interventions and therapies". There is no sign of such holistic thinking in the Government response.

7.   It is also unfortunate that the response purports to identify as the first main theme of our Report "the need for additional funding for research into the scientific aspects of ageing". In reality, out of over 40 recommendations in our Report, just one specifically made the case for such additional funding: our call for a significant increase in the £1.3 million spent by the Economic and Social Research Council on ageing research.[5]

8.   Indeed, we expressly refrained from making recommendations which would involve a major new injection of funds because we recognised that significant sums are already being expended on the health and well-being of older people, and that this is to the credit of Government. A more careful reading of our Report would have revealed a different "main theme": that better investment of existing resources could and would bring better returns.

9.   Our witnesses, some of the most eminent in their fields, gave us numerous examples of ways in which major benefits could be obtained with minimal expenditure—sometimes even with a saving of resources. There may of course be matters which we or our witnesses overlooked, or there may be cogent reasons—medical, ethical, technological, practical, financial or other—why a particular recommendation could not be accepted. But this is not what this unhelpfully defensive response tells us. Too often it simply lists all the existing Government initiatives in the relevant field, the implication being that because a lot is being done, all must be for the best, and no improvement can be possible.

10.   We set out below a few areas where the response has conspicuously failed to engage with our recommendations.

Healthy Life Expectancy

11.   Professor Sally Davies, the Director of Research and Development at the Department of Health, told us that healthy life expectancy (HLE) was growing more slowly than life expectancy (LE), so that there was an increase in the years of ill-health of older people. We noted that, if true, this was a

---

[5] First Report, paragraphs 8.28–8.29. The response (paragraph 112) refers to the £5.4m committed to the New Dynamics of Ageing project. As it states, this is "future spend"; we understand that none of it has yet been allocated to research.

matter for considerable concern.[6] However we received other evidence, suggesting that matters were not so simple, that the perceived increase in unhealthy life expectancy might not reflect a true increase, and that a better measure than HLE might be disability-free life expectancy.[7] We recommended that the Office for National Statistics (ONS) should carry out further research on this.

12.   The Government, after reviewing different measures of HLE, cite one ONS piece of research which shows that "people, despite living longer, can also expect to live more years in poor health". Yet the ONS themselves conceded in evidence to our inquiry that "concerns remain about the reliability of subjective assessments ... These are known to vary systematically across population sub-groups ... (reflecting) differences in ill-health, behaviour, expectations and cultural norms for health".[8] No such nuances are found in the response, which continues: "In other words, although healthy life expectancy is increasing, it is doing so more slowly than overall life expectancy".[9]

13.   This statement is made without any suggestion that it is either a cause for concern, or that any remedial action is needed. It flies in the face of the claim by Professor Ian Philp, the National Director for Older People's Health, in a report published in November 2004, that "Health in old age is improving and should continue to improve".[10] Nor do the Government comment on our suggestion that, given that 38 per cent of NHS expenditure is spent on the 16 per cent of the population over 65, anything which can be done to narrow the gap between LE and HLE will free significant resources.[11]

Stroke

14.   One recommendation, which would be particularly simple and inexpensive to implement, would be to place scanners for strokes in A&E departments to enable CT scans to be performed in hours rather than days. We received convincing evidence that conducting a scan immediately after a stroke has been diagnosed has a dramatic impact upon patient outcomes, helping to bring mortality rates down, and increasing the proportion of stroke patients who survive without serious disability. This would in turn bring enormous financial benefits—although, as the Stroke Research Network point out, such benefits have been neglected hitherto, possibly because "the financial benefits of acute stroke units and treatments are accrued by community services but the costs fall on hospital Trusts".

15.   We also referred[12] to an investigation then being carried out by the National Audit Office (NAO). The NAO Report, published on 16 November 2005,[13] supported our recommendation in every particular:

---

6 First Report, paragraphs 2.19–2.20.

7 First Report, paragraphs 2.20–2.28. The ONS evidence is at paragraphs 2.20–2.21.

8 First Report, paragraph 2.20.

9 Government Response, p. 2.

10 *Better Health in Old Age*, Department of Health, November 2004: see First Report, paragraphs 7.8–7.11.

11 First Report, paragraph 2.31.

12 First Report, paragraph 4.13.

13 *Reducing Brain Damage: Faster access to better health care*, Report by the Comptroller and Auditor General, Session 2005–06, HC 452. See in particular paragraphs 1.16–1.22.

"Only 22 per cent of stroke patients in the Sentinel Audit received a scan on the same day as their stroke. Most waited two or more days. For patients who were registered as requiring an urgent CT scan (within 30 minutes), only 30 per cent actually got the scan on the same day. But nearly all hospitals (91 per cent) have the capacity to be able to provide CT scans within 24 hours of admission. This means that scans for stroke patients are being delayed, even though 'time lost is brain lost'." (paragraph 1.18)

16.   The Government's response is to say that DoH has convened a Stroke Strategy Group. This Group is "developing work mapping the ideal patient care pathways for transient ischaemic attack and stroke. It is now working through the implementation challenges for the NHS, including how to ensure more rapid access to scans and maximise existing scanning capacity".[14] In the absence of clear measurable targets this sounds like a recipe for bureaucratic inaction. We urge the Government to reconsider.

Winter Mortality

17.   Excess winter mortality, primarily of older people, is a major problem in the United Kingdom. We therefore recommended that Government departments should work together to prepare "detailed plans" to eliminate the problem. The response merely repeats that the Government has a "Plan for Action", to eliminate fuel poverty in vulnerable households in England by 2010 (p. 8). In contrast, the Government-sponsored but independent Fuel Poverty Advisory Group (FPAG), in its 3rd Annual Report, said of this Action Plan: "This is, however, not a plan. There is no estimate of the resources required, no timeline to meet the 2010 and 2016 statutory fuel poverty targets, no consideration of the major obstacles and no assessment of the options available for overcoming them."[15]

18.   In particular, we urged the Government to take forward urgently the review of Part M of the Building Regulations, and to incorporate an updated version of the "Lifetime Home Standards". The background to this recommendation was as follows:

- In 1999 ODPM accepted the report of the Joseph Rowntree Trust advocating incorporating the Lifetime Homes Standards into Part M of the Building Regulations.

- On 10 March 2004 Phil Hope MP, the minister then responsible, announced to a House of Commons Select Committee a review of Building Regulations; the press notice said that "new standards could be in place in two years' time".

- In March 2005 *Opportunity Age*, the Government's strategy for older people, said that the review was undertaken "with a view to legislating by 2007 to incorporate the Lifetime Home Standards".[16]

19.   The Government's response to our recommendation was to state that "Lifetime Homes Standards will be a component of some levels of the Code for Sustainable Buildings." This Code, which is intended to come into effect by April 2006, "points the way for possible future Building Regulations and

---

[14] Government Response, p. 7.

[15] Third Annual Report, page 5. See http://www.dti.gov.uk/energy/consumers/fuel_poverty/fuel_adv_grp.shtml.

[16] *Opportunity Age*, paragraph 3.19. See http://www.dss.gov.uk/opportunity_age/.

is a practical way of incentivising adoptions of the standards."[17] Yet the Code will be voluntary: without amendment of the Building Regulations, and with no firm assurance that such amendment will be made in future, there is no guarantee that the Code will have any effect at all. Eight years after the Government accepted the recommendation of the Rowntree Report, the ministerial undertaking to legislate seems to have been quietly dropped.

Co-ordination of Research

20. Our main recommendation for improving the output of ageing research without a major injection of new resources centred on the co-ordination of this research. We reviewed four existing bodies and programmes charged with co-ordinating research, among them the Funders' Forum, and concluded that all had serious shortcomings. We argued that while DWP might be able to co-ordinate macro-policy on ageing, research should be the responsibility of OST. We recommended the establishment of a new body with the membership, constitution, powers and funding necessary to provide the strategic oversight and direction of ageing research.[18]

21. The Government "agree that there is a need to improve the level of co-ordination", but are "not convinced that a new body is needed". Instead they believe that this task should be allocated to the Funders' Forum. They "accept that the Forum has yet to fully deliver its objectives", but state that improvements are planned or under way which will revitalise the Forum.[19]

22. This would be acceptable if there was any evidence that the "improvements" would be adequate to transform the Funders' Forum into something resembling the body we recommended. But this is not what is proposed. We recommended that DTI and OST should be responsible, with the Chief Scientific Adviser playing a part. Instead, it is suggested that DoH should continue to be responsible for the Forum. We argued that the body would need dedicated funding. Instead, we are told that the Forum's secretariat will be financed by a "subscription" pledged by "the research councils, health departments and some charities". We criticised the Forum for never meeting. There is no suggestion that the "revitalised" body will meet more than occasionally—on 24 February this year it met for the first time since June 2003.

23. Dr James Goodwin, the Head of Research at Help the Aged, had told us that the Funders' Forum "has been perceived as lacking leadership, coherence and unified and purposeful effort".[20] We deduced from this that much of the success of the new body would depend on its being directed by the right person, and that "initially at least this may need to be a full-time post". Dr Goodwin has now himself been appointed as Director of the Forum, albeit part-time, to plan its future operation and strategy. He is also one of the principal authors of Help the Aged's additional written evidence, which contains a scathing indictment of the Government's "lamentable failure" to produce a clear strategy for the future of ageing research.

---

[17] Government Response, p. 9.

[18] First Report, paragraphs 8.40–8.58, 8.70–8.89.

[19] Government Response, p. 17.

[20] First Report, paragraph 8.46.

24. Help the Aged list various reasons why the initiatives so far undertaken by the Government "are insufficient in themselves to 'transform' the co-ordination of research". Prominent among these are that the Forum's recommendations will not be binding on the funding or strategy decisions of its members, and that it will have no direct or formal relationship with any Department of State. The authors conclude: "It is our view that a much more coherent and integrated approach by Government is necessary to bring together the apparent disparate initiatives of the various departments ... In summary, we find the Government's position on research coordination to be untenable, lacking in vision and without any clear and substantial plan for the future."[21]

25. Help the Aged would, understandably, like to see more resources devoted to ageing-related research. But we stress once more that this was not our recommendation. What we are seeking to achieve is better use of the resources already invested in ageing research—in particular, the resources invested on behalf of the taxpayer by the research councils. In light of the damning comments of Help the Aged, and the Director of the Funders' Forum, on the Government response, we hope it is not too late for Ministers to see sense.

Conclusion

26. We have described above a few areas where the Government response is particularly disappointing. However, similar objections could be raised to many other parts of the response, and many such points can be found in the written comments from our witnesses and from Professor Kirkwood.

27. At the same time, some progress has been made. We have, for example, received written comments from the British Council for Ageing (BCA), which brings together three learned societies with an interest in ageing, namely the British Society of Gerontology, the British Geriatrics Society and the British Society for Research on Ageing. The BCA was formed "as a direct result of the suggestion made by their Lordships that a single and readily identifiable point of contact for policy makers would be helpful",[22] and we are delighted that our recommendations on the co-ordination of research are being taken forward in this way by those at the cutting edge.

28. But without Government leadership progress will inevitably be limited—as the BCA comment, "without firm political direction from Government ... the problems ... will prove extremely difficult to remedy". It is not too late for the Government to provide this direction, though the signs are not encouraging.

29. A debate on our Report is forthcoming, and we hope to receive a more satisfactory response from the Minister in reply to that debate. But we also put on record our intention not to let these matters rest, but to continue to press the Government for action, if necessary by means of a further inquiry.

---

[21] Memorandum from Help the Aged, p 40.

[22] Memorandum from the BCA, p 20.

Written Evidence

GOVERNMENT RESPONSE TO THE HOUSE OF LORDS SCIENCE AND TECHNOLOGY COMMITTEE REPORT AGEING: SCIENTIFIC ASPECTS

INTRODUCTION

1. The Government welcomes the First Report of the Lords Science and Technology Committee, Session 2005–06, "Ageing: Scientific Aspects" which was published on 21 July 2005.

2. The Committee made a number of recommendations, but the main themes are: the need for additional funding for research into the scientific aspects of ageing; giving scientific aspects a higher priority in the consideration of ageing issues; improved co-ordination of research across the research councils; and a greater willingness by industry to embrace the opportunities that existing technologies offer for improving older people's quality of life.

3. The Government's view is that a great deal of progress has been made on all these fronts, but that there is more that can be done.

4. Starting with funding: the Government already invests heavily into research on ageing, including the scientific aspects. Whilst there may be a case for more investment, the Committee will recognise that, given finite resources, there will always be a need to balance competing priorities for research. Investment in research on ageing may need to be made (ultimately) at the expense of research in other areas of the life cycle, for example, such as birth, early years development, childhood and adolescence. Even within the arena of ageing-related research itself, there will be competing demands on funding for work on specific conditions/diseases associated with ageing against more generic work on the underlying mechanisms of the ageing process. To an extent, this tension is reflected in the Committee's own recommendations which suggest that more should be done on the latter (9.12) but which also emphasise the importance of investment in research on specific conditions such as stroke/cancer.

5. Government, research councils and others are prepared to fund research, but delivery remains subject to worthwhile projects being proposed by competent researchers.

6. In addition, against work on the biological process of ageing or on specific diseases/conditions associated with ageing, there is also a need to understand more about the non-biophysical factors affecting the ageing process, the psychosocial experiences of different ageing sub-populations and the impact of health and welfare services provided to older people and their families. Inevitably prioritisation has to take place and will involve the need to balance the different, and often competing, views of scientists, professionals, older people and their organisations as well as society more widely. It is important to take this wider context into account in assessing how well individual funding bodies, Departments or the Government as a whole, perform against specific areas of scientific interest.

7. The Government agrees that there is a need for an improved level of co-ordination across all funders of research relating to ageing, and believes that structures are being put in place to properly ensure this will happen in the future.

8. On the question of industry making the best of existing technology, as the Committee itself notes, that is largely a matter for industry itself, but the Government acknowledges that it has a part to play, not least in helping to shift cultural attitudes to ageing. Our strategy, as set out in *Opportunity Age*, focuses heavily on these cultural aspects. Specifically, the Government will write to the key organisations mentioned in paragraph 9.28 of the Report recommendations.

9. In conclusion, the Government thinks that the Committee has raised important issues and agrees that there are significant challenges to harness the opportunities that science offers to improve the well-being of older people. However, the Government is confident that it is addressing those issues and challenges. The Government will be happy to continue liaising with the Committee on developments. In addition, the Government has made the Committee's report available to the Devolved Administrations who will have regard to the helpful evidence and conclusions when developing policies related to ageing.

10. The Government's response to each of the Committee's conclusions and recommendations is set out in the following section.

CONCLUSIONS AND RECOMMENDATIONS

Paragraphs 9.3-9.5

Demographic Change

9.3. At current rates, life expectancy within the UK is increasing at the rate of about two years for each decade that passes. The consequences of this demographic change for all aspects of life are profound. As this Report will show, we have found little evidence that policy has been sufficiently informed by scientific understanding of the ageing process.

9.4. We conclude that there is considerable uncertainty about whether healthy lifespan is increasing faster or slower than lifespan. The uncertainty comes from the variability in individual health trajectories through life, and the difficulty in applying objective measures of health and quality of life across different age groups. We believe that freedom from disability provides a more easily ascertainable objective measure of the quality of life.

9.5. Further research should be undertaken to validate and apply appropriate measures to monitor the trends in healthy lifespan. We recommend that funds should be made available to the Office for National Statistics to enable it to carry out over a number of years the surveys needed to assess disability-free life expectancy.

ONS is the key provider of demographic data on ageing and is engaged in work to analyse the demographic implications of ageing. Key strands of the work include investigating the demographic characteristics and living arrangements of older people in the UK and also the relationship between demographic characteristics and care arrangements in old age. ONS aims to combine information from the best available data sources on the older population and to produce statistics that provide an objective basis for policy, particularly for those aged 85 and over who are the fastest growing age group.

In this context, ONS has set up a pensions statistics taskforce whose primary purpose is to produce improved pension statistics, but which also draws together health, economic and demographic data in relation to issues surrounding pension provision.

Information on health trajectories tends to be measured in terms of illness or disease and, in some respects, these can be regarded as more factual than measures of disability. On the other hand disability, which covers "activity limitations and participation restrictions" (according to the International Classification of Functioning, WHO 2001) is more relevant to quality of life than general health but has to be seen as only one domain of quality of life among several others.

Data on freedom from disability is most often obtained by responses to questions in censuses and national surveys on limiting, longstanding illness. Asking respondents to say whether their health problem is limiting adds a subjective element to the assessment. Thus available survey measures of disability are not objective but, like other simple questions on health status, have consistently been found to be a good predictor of subsequent survival. Respondents have also been found to under-report mental health problems and chronic, but episodic, conditions.

Taken together, the indicators currently produced by ONS, based on disability and perceived general health, provide a rounded picture of how many of the extra years of life among an ageing population are affected by ill-health or other functional limitations. They should not be seen as alternative measures of quality of life.

Figures based on limiting longstanding illness cover the widest range of disabilities. But, as this is a subjective question, these may be more strongly linked to changes in the social environment. Currently there is no consistent, regular series looking at trends in severe forms of disability, (with an inability to carry out personal tasks independently being regarded as the extreme end of the functional limitation scale).

The question on limiting long-term illness (LLTI) was included in the 1991 and 2001 Censuses and is being considered again for the 2011 Census. The question is also included in many of the continuous surveys carried out by ONS. Specifically, it is included in the General Household Survey and this is the source currently used to produce trends on disability-free life expectancy.

ONS publishes figures relating to healthy life expectancy on both bases, that is using questions on general health and on limiting long-term illness. Latest results on healthy life expectancy (HLE), published in 2004, show that for both indicators: "total life expectancy continues to increase steadily and at a faster rate than healthy life expectancy meaning that people, despite living longer, can also expect to live more years in poor health".[1] In other words, although healthy life expectancy is increasing, it is doing so more slowly than overall life expectancy.

---

[1] ONS (2004) Healthy Life Expectancy in Great Britain: 2001. Health statistics Quarterly, 23, 75–77.

The question on limiting longstanding illness is also included in the three questions which comprise the Minimum European Health Module and is included in the EU Survey of Income and Living Conditions (SILC) which is implemented by ONS in the UK under EU regulations. Questions from EU-SILC will also be used by Eurostat to provide the estimate of Healthy Life Years which is proposed in a new set of structural indicators for the EU. This will aid comparability across Europe in the measurement of health expectancy, which will further increase our scientific understanding of how the ageing process is impacting on demographic transition.

Promoting Good Health: Physical Activity

9.6. Local authorities can do much to help people of all ages, including older people, to benefit from exercise. Facilities for cycling are often poor or non-existent; sometimes even walking is a perilous activity. Local authorities should aim to improve facilities for exercise; they should make it their business to inform older people about these facilities; they should encourage them to use these facilities; and they should ensure that adequate transport is available.

The Government agrees that local authorities can contribute much to help people of all ages benefit from exercise. It is proposed that the redesigned Comprehensive Performance Assessment (CPA), including the cultural services assessment, will measure achievements in increasing participation in sport and physical activity and ensuring that facilities are accessible to all.

Separately, the corporate services assessment will examine whether sport and physical activity are being used effectively in relation to national or local priorities like social inclusion, safer communities and social cohesion. For the first time, national and local performance data will be available to help identify areas where improvement is most needed, so that local authorities, The Department for Culture, Media and Sport (DCMS) and its partners can focus their support. Some other performance indicators that will help authorities focus on increasing participation include; ease of use of public footpaths, residents' satisfaction with facilities, levels of participation in sport and recreational walking related to the population distribution in the area (different social classes, ethnic origin and age groups—including over 60's are sampled) volunteering, travel time to good quality facilities and how well local facilities are used. All of these will be included by 2006.

The Government acknowledges that one of the obstacles preventing people from playing sport is a lack of good sports facilities. By 2006, the Government and the National Lottery will have committed over £1 billion to develop new or refurbished sports facilities. Over 80 per cent of that money has already been committed or spent on a wide range of facilities programmes. This represents a considerable investment in our sports facilities infrastructure.

The "Active Places" web-site, launched in July 2004, provides a comprehensive picture of sports facilities across the country, which are open to the general public, making it easier for people to find sports facilities in their area. In March 2005, the Active Places web-site was enhanced by "Active Places Power". This was designed to help local authorities and sports organisations to identify gaps in sports facility provision and to form strategies for sports facility investment.

Looking to the future, the Government wants to help local authorities to revitalise their leisure facilities and to ensure that the right sports facilities are in the right places. The Government plans to develop a comprehensive facilities strategy mapping out supply, demand and priorities for investment. The aim is that, by 2008, the majority of people will live within 20 minutes of a good multi-sports environment, such as a school, sports club or leisure centre. The Department for Culture, Media and Sport and the Office for the Deputy Prime Minister will work together to ensure that sports facilities planning guidance is rigorous, fit for purpose and free from unnecessary barriers.

The Audit Commission will also undertake a study of local authority facilities to examine the scope for efficiencies and identify standards of good practice that can be disseminated and employed across the country. The Audit Commission study is expected to be publicly available in early 2006.

In the meantime, the Government is continuing with its wider agenda to promote exercise. The Department for Transport published *"Walking and Cycling: an action plan"*[2] in June 2004. The report contained more than 40 measures being taken across Government to improve the provision for and promotion of walking and cycling. Highlights included development of a new national standard for cycle training, new training for transport practitioners, professionals on catering for pedestrian and cyclists' needs in the design process.

---

[2] Available from the Department of Transport Publications Centre, Tel 0870 1226 236 or e-mail dft@twoten.press.net Product Code TNF931.

The Government set out in Planning Policy Guidance Note 13: Transport (DETR 2001), guidance to promote accessibility to jobs, shopping, leisure facilities and services by walking and cycling and the creation of an environment which takes account of the needs of disabled people. Policy Statement 6: Planning for Town Centres (PPS6–ODPM, 2005), advises local authorities to encourage the use of walking and cycling, and to consider access by such modes when allocating sites for development. PPS6 also advises that when assessing planning applications, local authorities should consider whether access to proposed developments is easy, safe and convenient for pedestrians, cyclists and disabled people.

The Action Plan reaffirms the needs of disabled people, such as using non-slip paving, installing more dropped kerbs, removing street clutter and clear signage. The Department for Transport is also looking for better transport planning through the Local Transport Plan (LTP) process where local authorities are expected to set out in their plans how their policies will deliver better outcomes for congestion, pollution and road safety and improve quality of life and health. Final LTPs for 2006–11 are due to be submitted by the end of March 2006.

The Department for Transport is showcasing best practice for encouraging cycling and walking, mainly by providing improved infrastructure and intensive marketing campaigns in three sustainable travel towns, Peterborough, Darlington and Worcester. The Department for Transport is investing £10 million over the next five years and will act as "models" for the promotion of sustainable travel. It will also improve street lighting by encouraging local authorities to consider using the option of using Private Finance Initiative (PFI) to fund improvements. Ten local authority street lighting schemes have been procured through PFI with a further 10 going through the procurement process;

The Action Plan will assist in improving the local cycle networks which will help reduce cycling on the pavement and well designed off road routes such as the National Cycling Network can also benefit pedestrians including elderly and disabled people.

The Department for Transport has also created a new expert advisory body, Cycling England, to plan and co-ordinate cycling across the country. Cycling England is supported and directed by a cross-Government group, which includes representatives from these Departments: Transport, Office of Deputy Prime Minister, Health, Education and Skills, Environment, Food and Regional Affairs and Culture, Media and Sport (Sport England).

The Department for Transport continues to work with the leading Non-Government Organisations (NGOs) (Living Streets, The Ramblers, Walk 21, Sustrans) on promoting walking and cycling to the population as a whole, including older people.

Promotion of walking and cycling is key to increasing the number of journeys by both modes. As part of the Department of Transport, sustainable travel demonstration towns project, Worcester, Peterborough and Darlington are undertaking comprehensive programmes of personalised travel planning (PTP). This includes direct marketing of walking and cycling information to households across each town and also assists in the promotion of safe and pleasant travel on town-wide basis.

9.7. Exercise at all ages is one of the most effective ways to counter the adverse effects of ageing on functional capacity. The Government should publish plans showing how they intend to promote, in schools and elsewhere, the benefits of exercise as a factor contributing to improved health at all ages.

The Government recognises the importance of physical activity in helping to counter the adverse effects of ageing on functional capacity. The health benefits of physical activity across the life-course have been set out in the Chief Medical Officer's Report *At least five a week*. The Chief Medical Officer's recommendation for adults to achieve a total of at least 30 minutes a day of at least moderate intensity physical activity on five or more days of the week extends to older adults. The report recommends that older people take particular care to keep moving and retain their mobility through daily activity. Additionally, specific activities that promote improved strength, co-ordination and balance are particularly beneficial for older people.

In March 2005, the Government published *Choosing Activity: a physical activity action plan*[3] to bring together all the commitments relating to physical activity in *Choosing Health*[4] as well as further activity across Government, which will contribute to increasing levels of physical activity. It provides further detail on both the context, and next steps, for action at national, regional and local levels to improve people's health through participation in physical activity.

In addition, and specifically aimed at younger people, the National Physical Education, School Sport and Club Links (PESSCL) strategy was introduced from April 2003. The overall objective is to increase the percentage of 5–16 year-olds who spend a minimum of two hours each week on high quality PE and School

---

[3] http://www.dh.gov.uk/PublicationsAndStatistics.
[4] Cm 6374, November 2004.

Sport, within and beyond the curriculum, to 75 per cent by 2006. By 2008, the aim is to raise this to 85 per cent with all children being offered entitlement. Also by 2008 the Government wants all school sport partnerships and families of schools working together to enhance school sport to enable at least 75 per cent of their pupils to take up this entitlement.

Promoting greater participation in physical activity for children is also a key component of the Government's Public Service Agreement (PSA) on childhood obesity. The PSA is the first high level response to this major public health challenge, committing Government to halting the year-on-year rise in obesity among children aged under 11 by 2010 in the context of a broader strategy to tackle obesity in the population as a whole. In recognition that meeting the target will depend on joined-up working across Government and locally, the target is owned jointly by the Department of Health, the Department for Education and Skills and the Department for Culture, Media and Sport.

9.8. Consent for the disposal of playing fields must be refused unless the facilities lost are to be replaced by sports or exercise facilities which are as good or better.

Through its national planning guidance to local authorities and other legislative measures introduced in 1998, the Government requires local authorities to protect playing fields and other forms of open space that their communities need. In July 2005, the Government released figures on the number of planning applications relating to playing fields in England during 2003–04. These figures reveal that in that year, more new playing fields were created (72) than had been lost (52). In addition, of the 959 applications for playing fields development that had been approved, 590 involved development projects that would greatly improve the quality of sport on offer at the site. This included new sports centres, tennis courts and athletics tracks, as well as changing facilities and floodlights. A further 314 applications were approved for developments on land which, whilst located on playing fields, did not form part of a playing pitch and was too small an area to accommodate one. Such developments included extensions to classrooms and the siting of temporary classrooms. While these figures are encouraging, the Government recognises that there is always more to do, and it is continuing to work further to improve the protection afforded to playing fields.

On Playing Fields, the further work relates to the prevention of demolition of sports facilities located on playing fields, and the reduction of the definition of playing fields from 0.4 hectares to 0.2 hectares.

Nutrition

9.9. Nutrition and oral health have major impacts on health throughout the lifespan. Since a person's health in old age reflects molecular and cellular damage that accumulates throughout life, and since nutrition affects the accumulation of such damage (adversely in the case of poor nutrition, beneficially in the case of good nutrition), the links between healthy eating and healthy ageing need to be better understood and communicated to the public.

The Government recognises the importance of healthy eating advice being communicated effectively to enable consumer understanding. A key role of the Food Standards Agency is to provide messages to help all consumers make informed choices about the food and drinks they purchase and consume.

To communicate healthy eating messages effectively the Agency recognises and reflects the sometimes diverse demands of consumers. It is with this in mind that the Agency has adopted a multi-faceted approach, using a variety of different styles and routes of communication to enable behaviour change.

The Agency's website "Eatwell" and written resources are a major source of comprehensive information for consumers on all aspects of diet, nutrition and health. There has been a growth in access to materials, especially through increasing use of the website since its launch in October 2004.

The Department of Health is funding a number of studies on the impact of lifestyle factors, including nutrition, on the health of ageing populations. Both MRC and BBSRC have ongoing research focused on the role of nutrition in health, including the prevention of chronic ailments and on the epidemiology and molecular aetiology of nutrition in cancer prevention and survival. And BBSRC is working towards the establishment of a priority area on *diet, exercise and health during ageing*.

The National Prevention Research Initiative (NPRI) launched in October 2004 is addressing the role of diet and nutrition. The Initiative is sponsored by a broad cross-section of funders, including research councils and the Health Departments. The NPRI is focused on the primary prevention of cancer, coronary heart disease and diabetes. Research projects will amongst other things address the role of diet and nutrition and will have direct relevance to reducing risk and influencing health behaviours. The full applications currently being considered include a number which focus on physical activity as a behavioural intervention in older people and the elderly.

9.10. We welcome and commend the approach of the White Paper *Choosing Health,* **and the importance it attaches to the provision of information about healthy nutrition. We recommend that this approach should be extended to cover the specific problems of older people.**

The Government supports the Committee's recommendation that healthy nutrition information should cover the specific problems of older people. Targeted practical and informative healthy eating advice for older people is provided on the Food Standards Agency's website "Eatwell". The Agency also produces this information as a leaflet, "Eating for later life".

The National Service Framework for Older People, launched in March 2001, has a specific standard on healthy active ageing and, as such, recognises the importance of improving diet and nutrition. *Choosing Health* provides us with another opportunity to promote this message.

Promoting healthy active life in old age is one of the 12 priorities in the White Paper's Delivery Plan. The promotion of health amongst older people was also a priority in the Green Paper consultation document "Independence, Well-being and Choice, the Government's vision for adult social care". These policy documents provide a framework for the NHS and local government to work in closer partnership in improving the health, independence and well-being of older people.

Individuality of the Ageing Process

9.11. In the light of improved knowledge of underlying biological mechanisms and the need to measure the efficacy of interventions aimed at improving healthy ageing, we recommend that specific attention be given to funding research on biomarkers of ageing.

Biomarkers for ageing are potentially important tools to enable us to disentangle "functional age" from chronological age so that for example the use of the mouse model system (mice normally live for between two and three years) might be more easily related to humans. Biomarkers also make it more easy to assess the impact of experimental manipulations on the ageing process in a realistic time period (ie does the experimental manipulation increase, decrease or have no impact on the functional age of the organism?).

The MRC is already in the process of considering how the UK can contribute to the broad field of biomarkers, not just in the area of ageing. This is in partnership with the BBSRC and the Wellcome Trust, and also involving industry. The shift towards a more holistic approach to the study of health and disease provides new impetus for developing the science of biomarkers, and there are considerable opportunities for exploitation and translation into improved health. Dramatic advances in "-omics" technologies have led to high expectations for the emergence of a new range of biomarkers, providing deeper insight into the behaviour of disease and response to drugs. As a first step, the MRC is holding a two-day meeting on biomarkers in January 2006 designed to address the extent to which this expectation can be met and identify how the UK can best contribute to the strong international effort in this area through capitalising on its infrastructure and scientific strengths. The workshop has a focus on disease, including cardiovascular and neurodegenerative disease, but is also likely to touch on biomarkers of ageing. The MRC will consider the recommendations of the workshop in February 2006 in the context of financial planning for 2006–07 and beyond, and it is likely to result in a call for proposals.

BBSRC funding of ageing research has concentrated on understanding the underlying biological mechanisms of ageing but has recently incorporated studies on biomarkers as part of their overall contribution to understanding ageing. An example of this approach is BBSRC's specific advice to applicants to the New Dynamics of Ageing (NDA) Programme which highlighted biomarkers of ageing as a one example of research that could be included in any applications to the initiative.

9.12. Most of the research on ageing and health within the UK is focused on specific diseases and medical conditions for which age is the single largest risk factor. However, there is little research on underpinning mechanisms of such diseases which may be linked to basic processes of ageing. The Department of Health and other medical research funders, including the major charities, should develop and implement strategies to address links between ageing and disease.

The Funders' Forum for Research into Ageing and Older People is planning to undertake a comprehensive portfolio analysis to identify priority areas for future funding. The Government will ensure that the Committee's recommendation is taken into account during this prioritisation exercise. It is intended that the Forum will analyse the portfolio across all public and private sector funders of ageing research, building on the preliminary portfolio analysis undertaken by the research councils, and the clinical research database being compiled by the UK Clinical Research Collaboration.

The Department of Health's central focus is on research to improve the delivery of NHS and social care services and maximise their impact on the health and well-being of older people. Other medical research funders will play a more central role in respect of the links between the basic processes of ageing and the underpinning mechanisms of diseases. The Department of Health will however seek to supplement and support this work wherever possible and actively contribute to the development of relevant collaborative strategies under the Funders' Forum.

Age-related Diseases

9.13. Stroke is a major cause of long-term illness, disability and death, particularly among older people. Yet significant reductions in the long-term health consequences of a stroke can be made if very early assessments and treatments are provided, for example by locating scanners within accident and emergency departments. The Department of Health should make rapid treatment of stroke a priority.

The Government recognised the importance of stroke by featuring it as a core standard of the Older People's National Service Framework (2001) and considerable progress has been made since then in the development of specialist stroke services, which were almost non-existent 10 years ago and are now present in almost every NHS Trust. In recent years, the evidence base for an emergency response to stroke has advanced significantly and the Department has responded by setting up a new stroke team and convening a Stroke Strategy Group. This stroke group, working under the auspices of the Department's new Vascular Programme Board, has been developing work mapping the ideal patient care pathways for transient ischaemic attack and stroke. It is now working through the implementation challenges for the NHS, including how to ensure more rapid access to scans and maximise existing scanning capacity.

9.14. We recommend that the Government and research councils should, when allocating money to cancer research, place more emphasis on those cancers particularly prevalent among the elderly. We encourage Cancer Research UK to do likewise.

The Government will ensure that the National Cancer Research Institute (NCRI) is aware of this recommendation. The incidence of many cancers, including the most common, rise markedly with age. To the extent that it is possible to view cancer in general as a disease of old age, research on cancer involving people at any age will be of benefit to older people. Moreover, much cancer research is strongly transferable. Analysis by the NCRI indicates that just under two thirds of all UK cancer research spend is relevant to all cancers.

Significant work is underway and planned in both MRC and the Department of Health on cancers which are particularly prevalent in the elderly, including cancers of the bowel, breast, prostate and lung. Three examples of past successes and current initiatives are described below.

— The NHS Bowel Cancer Screening Programme for individuals aged 60–69, which is to be phased in from April 2006, was a direct result of a major MRC-funded clinical trial. The screening test, called a faecal occult blood test, is used to detect non-visible traces of blood in faeces. The trial showed that screening using this test can reduce the mortality rate from bowel cancer by 15 per cent in those screened.

— Under the auspices of the Cancer Research Funders' Forum (the forerunner of the National Cancer Research Institute, NCRI), the MRC carried out a review of the state of prostate cancer research in the UK in 2000–01. As a result of this the MRC took a leading role in establishing two "Prostate Cancer Research Collaboratives" with funding from several funders, with the aim to facilitate the development of a critical mass of research in prostate cancer. A review of progress and potential renewal of funding is now under consideration by the NCRI partners

— The Department of Health has commissioned research to examine early symptoms and the extent and causes of delay in presentation by patients. This will be likely to increase the proportion of the population "living well'" into older age.

Age-related Disorders

9.15. We recommend that the Department of Health should continue to take urgent steps to remedy the shortage of dentists, and to encourage a habit of more frequent check-ups, especially among older people.

The Government's programme for revitalising NHS dentistry is progressing well. The target set to recruit 1,000 whole time equivalent dentists by the end of October will be achieved. This will create the capacity for two million more people to see an NHS dentist. For the longer term, the number of undergraduate training place in dentistry has been increased by 170 (25 per cent).

New contractual arrangements will be in place in April 2006 which will help retain dentists within the NHS. They will provide for dentists to broaden their expertise into preventing dental disease. At the same time a new charging system will be introduced with which it is intended to replace the previous complicated system made up of over 400 charges with three simplified bands. Patients on low income will continue to be exempt from dental charges.

9.16. Older people are disproportionately affected by many specific diseases and sensory impairments, and the expenditure directed at these diseases appears to be far lower than would be expected. A population with a growing number of older people will result in an increasing burden on society from some conditions for which age is a significant risk factor.

While the Government acknowledges that age is a significant risk factor for some diseases, the relationship is not necessarily constant over time or between. A major component of health care costs is known to be related to proximity to death. For these reasons, changes in the burden of health care and associated costs cannot be predicted simply from demographic information.

However, when considering expenditure directed at specific diseases and sensory impairment, the costs of treatment in hospitals, GP consultations, or prescribed medication represent only one type of expenditure. Limitations in functioning and activity restrictions also have an economic as well as a societal cost. Meeting the needs of people with health problems is dependent both on their capacity to perform daily tasks as well as their health status. Trends in disability-free life expectancy will therefore have a stronger influence on burden than demographic change alone.

9.17. The Government should re-examine their research priorities, and promote expenditure on research into the alleviation of those conditions which disproportionately affect older people.

Priorities for the Science Budget are set as part of each Spending Review following discussions between the Office of Science and Technology (OST) and Research Councils, and are then reflected in Councils spending plans. The Spending Review 2004 allocations were aligned with the Government's Science and Innovation investment framework 2004–14, published in July 2004, which outlined the Government's long-term vision for UK science. The next Spending Review will take place in 2007 and this will give OST and Councils an opportunity to set new priorities.

OST will undertake an early review of overall Research Council investment in research relating to ageing and its alignment with funding from other sources. OST will ensure that in future Spending Review bids and allocations the Research Council programmes will be coherent both internally and with other funders.

As is described in the response to recommendations 9.41 to 9.48 below, both the Government Chief Scientific Adviser's Committee (CSAC) and the Coordination of Research and Analysis Group (CRAG) have concluded that ageing is a priority for the Government as a whole.

The Built Environment

9.18. The Office of the Deputy Prime Minister and the Department of Health should join with the Department for the Environment, Food and Rural Affairs and the Department of Trade and Industry in pressing ahead with the preparation of detailed plans for the elimination of deaths of older people caused by cold and damp, and should provide the resources to implement these plans.

In response to the introduction of the Warm Homes and Energy Conservation Act 2000, the Government developed its own *Fuel Poverty Strategy*,[5] which set out a range of programmes across the UK to reduce the number of households in fuel poverty, recognising that the issue needs to be tackled on a number of fronts and with the engagement of a wide range of stakeholders. Setting targets for the eradication of fuel poverty, the Strategy helped the focus to be on action. Fuel Poverty in England: The Government's Plan for Action[6] sets out the wide range of policies aiming to eradicate fuel poverty as far as reasonably practicable amongst vulnerable households, including the elderly, by 2010. The Government's *Third Annual Progress Report*[7] published earlier this year, describes the progress being made. The Office of the Deputy Prime Minister and the Department of Health make important contributions to this progress.

The Department of Health is actively collaborating with other government departments on a wide range of fronts to reduce excess winter mortality. The contribution to the eradication of fuel poverty is an important part of this. Specific policies and actions include:

---

[5] The UK Fuel Poverty Strategy Third Annual Progress Report, 2005, published by Defra, DTI, DSD, Scottish Executive and Welsh Assembly Government, URN 05/353 available at http://www.dti.gov.uk/energy/consumers/fuel_poverty/fuel_strategy.shtml

[6] www.defraweb/environment/energy/fuelpov/pdf/fuelpov_actionplan.pdf

[7] www.dti.gov.uk/energy/consumers/fuel_poverty/strategy_third_progress_report.pdf

— Flu and pneumococcal immunisation programmes. The UK has the highest uptake of flu immunisation among eligible groups of any in Europe.

— The Keep Warm Keep Well Campaign, launched this year with the Flu immunisation campaign, comprising leaflet and help-line based advice on what simple measures older people can take to preserve their health in winter time. Advice on how to access Warm Front and other fuel poverty reducing agencies is part of this.

— Direct encouragement to the NHS to increase further the many fuel poverty reduction partnerships between the NHS, local authorities and, for example, EAGA. These lead to primary care staff being trained and supported, simplified referral routes and rapid response from Warm Front and others. It is worth noting that the overwhelming majority of referrals to Warm Front originate from the NHS.

— Funding the evaluation of an important collaboration between the NHS and the Met Office, testing the value of health forecasting in the management and self-management of those with chronic chest disease, many of whom are older people.

— Helping to set up the Health, Housing and Fuel Poverty forum in March 2005 to raise the profile of cold, damp homes and to mainstream the many innovative activities the NHS is engaged in to address this issue.

— Establishing the £60 million "Partnerships for Older People Projects" fund, against which local authorities and their partners have been bidding this year. The focus of these projects is on improving outcomes for older people through preventive interventions. Fuel poverty reduction forms a part of several of the short listed bids.

The Office of the Deputy Prime Minister's (ODPM) programme for all social sector homes in England meet the Decent Homes Standard (DHS) by 2010 continues to contribute to the alleviation of fuel poverty in the social sector through improvements in stock condition. Energy efficiency improvements have been a major outcome of refurbishment works to deliver the DHS with the number of social homes failing to meet the thermal comfort criterion reduced by 20 per cent between 2001 and 2003. Significant improvements have also been made to improve living conditions for vulnerable households in the private sector. ODPM is committed to ensuring that energy efficiency is taken fully into account in the implementation of the new Housing Act 2004, which will enable housing conditions to be assessed specifically for their health and safety impact on tenants.

Departments are committed to contributing to the Government's collective drive to meet fuel poverty targets. For example, the Department for Work and Pensions made over 11.5 million Winter Fuel Payments last winter. Over 2.35 million customers aged 80 and over received the extra payment totalling over £212 million (£100 is paid to households with someone aged 80 or £50 each if there is more than one eligible 80 year old in the household).

9.19. We urge the Government to take forward urgently the review of Part M of the Building Regulations, to bring up to date the Lifetime Home Standards, and to amend the Regulations to incorporate the revised standards.

The Government is proposing that Lifetime Homes Standards will be a component of some levels of the Code for Sustainable Buildings. It is proposed that the Code will be published for consultation before Christmas and will come into effect by April 2006. The Code points the way for possible future Building Regulations and is a practical way of incentivising adoptions of the standards.

Transport

9.20. We recommend that, when reaching decisions on the review commissioned by the DVLA, the Department for Transport should not exclude the option of allowing licence-holders to determine for themselves the age at which they should cease to drive.

The Government has provided copies of the Committee's report to the company carrying out the independent review for DVLA drawing attention specifically to this recommendation. This will ensure that the recommendation that the option that licence holders should determine for themselves the age at which they should cease to drive is properly considered as part of that review. The report is expected in November 2005. The report from the review will be put into the public domain once consideration of the recommendations is complete. The current intention is to make the outcomes from the review the subject of a conference being organised by the Parliamentary Advisory Council on Transport Safety in February 2006. A public consultation on any changes is expected to be launched in the spring.

9.21. We believe the evidence clearly shows how older people enter into a negative spiral towards dependency through social isolation and inactivity, often founded on lack of access to suitable transport, amenities and opportunities for exercise.

The Government recognises and accepts the correlation between a loss of independent mobility and a decline in physical and mental well-being in older people. The improvements in access to public transport required under the Disability Discrimination Act are benefiting many older people as well as those who are disabled.

The Government has commissioned two pieces of research into facilities and services available to help older people continue to drive safely and at options for older people who give up driving. TTR Ltd was commissioned to review driving advice and assessment services for older drivers in the UK. The specific objectives of the research were to:

— identify and list all services offering advice to older drivers;

— report on how older drivers access these services;

— report on the methods for assessment and advice used by the services;

— report on the satisfaction of users of the services; and

— report on the satisfaction of organisations/professionals who use the services.

Professor Sandi Rosenbloom, an internationally recognised expert on ageing and driving, has been commissioned to investigate the reasons why older people give up driving, what the resulting personal and societal implications and costs are. As part of this project she will explore ways of ameliorating and supporting older people in this process which can lead to health problems, loneliness and isolation.

The Government is hoping for the following outputs:

— a report on the evidence on reasons, implications and costs;

— recommendations on possible interventions that help prolong safe driving in old age; and

— advice and guidance for older people on maintaining and improving their mobility in old age.

9.22. Government, local authorities, transport companies and service providers should plan on the assumption that the average age of users and the proportion of older users will continue to increase. Compliance with regulations requiring provision for older people should be monitored.

The Government is well aware of the demographic trends and the needs of the growing numbers of older people to remain mobile. In particular, the Department of Transport, is working closely with local authorities and others such as Strategic Health Authorities, NHS Trusts and Primary Care Trusts to ensure that older people's needs are built into the planning and delivery of local transport services and facilities.

Local authorities, particularly, will be expected to develop and deliver accessibility strategies as part of their next Local Transport Plans.[8] The Government issued Guidance[9] in December 2004 on accessibility planning, encouraging local authorities and their partners, to consider the different needs and problems of different sections of their local community, including older people, in accessing the services and facilities that they need. Local authorities themselves should evaluate and monitor their own action plans.

Communication

9.23. We believe that some of the most exciting opportunities for scientific advance to benefit older people arise through use of information technology. Industry self-regulation has notably failed to address these needs and opportunities.

The increasing call on the public purse of caring for an ageing population and the wish many older people have to remain in their own homes, has led the Government to engage with industry and the research base. In doing so it has supported collaborations such as The Application Home Initiative, that is developing an infrastructure to distribute services around the home. It has supported the Association of Social and Community Alarms providers (ASAP) and maintains close links with assistive technology players (Attendo, Tunstall, GE Healthcare) and the eHealth sector (BT, iSOFT) where solutions appropriate to home care of the elderly are developed.

The November 2004 Technology Programme competition encouraged collaborative R&D applications in Telecare, specifically technologies to stop the institutionalisation of elderly citizens allowing them to safely and happily remain in their own homes and those to address chronic diseases management. A number of quality proposals were received and relevant projects are now being taken forward.

---

[8] Full Guidance on Local Transport Plans, published December 2004.

[9] Guidance on Accessibility Planning in Local Transport Plans, published December 2004.

The Government has facilitated industry involvement in the Department of Health led Electronic Technologies Policy Collaborative, successfully concluding work on the regime for Preventative Technologies Grant (PTG) which will be available from April 2006. It has also supported industry awareness raising events such as the July 2005 Connected HomeCare conference hosted at CBI and is currently working with partners to ensure that PTG is successfully implemented from next year.

9.24. The Government's target should be that every home, including those in rural areas where social isolation of older people is often severe, should receive access to affordable high bandwidth IT connection within three years. If necessary, Ofcom should rely on its regulatory powers to secure this. Local authorities should offer older people training packages in the use of IT.

The UK has made remarkable progress in its coverage of high bandwidth IT connections. The UK has the most extensive broadband market in the G7 group of countries as at the end of June 2005 over 99.3 per cent of households are able to receive broadband and this is due to rise to over 99.6 per cent by the end of 2005.

The case for a Universal Service Obligation (USO) for broadband is not currently strong either on the basis of economic efficiency or of equity. It is too early in the development of the market for the necessary conditions to be met. The combination of BT's roll-out of DSL and its adoption of extended reach DSL, means that BT and market dynamics will make DSL available to 99.6 per cent of the population during 2005. The remaining shortfall is currently being addressed through public sector infrastructure schemes.

In its review of the scope of the USO, the European Commission reaches similar interim conclusions to Ofcom on broadband. The Commission's view is an extension of USO is not appropriate at this time as broadband is not used by the majority of consumers.

The Government has taken strong action to ensure that rural areas are not left behind in the rollout of broadband. In May 2003, The Department of Trade and Industry and the Department for Environment, Food and Rural Affairs (Defra) ministers created the DTI Rural Broadband Unit, to work across all levels of government to stimulate a sharper focus on the impact of broadband on rural economies. With the work largely complete the Rural Unit has since disbanded but there are still strong links between DTI Broadband team and Defra.

On the ground, local and regional initiatives involving devolved administrations in Northern Ireland, Scotland, Wales, the Regional Development Agencies in England and local authorities with other partners are helping many businesses and communities to take advantage of the benefits of broadband.

With the infrastructure largely in place, the UK is beginning a new phase of broadband take-up and higher bandwidth application. The UK is focusing on take-up and delivery of digital content and promoting social inclusion through publication of a Digital Strategy. The Government is committed to ensuring that **all** of society can benefit from Information Communication Technology (ICT): improved cohesion, economic wealth and quality of life.

In April 2005, the Government launched Connecting the UK: the Digital Strategy outlining the steps it is taking to close the digital divide between those with access to ICT and those without.

The People's Network, the £120 million Lottery Funded programme connected the 4,200 public libraries in the UK to the Internet. 90 per cent of these have broadband access. This represents a significant contribution to the Government's target of universal Internet access for UK citizens by 2005. 90 per cent of authorities signed up to free access and, where they do charge, the range tends to be between 50p—£3 an hour. Concessions for particular groups, including seniors, are generally offered. This enables vulnerable groups to maintain contact with friends and family, to access on-line services through websites such as Directgov and their local authority website, start new hobbies, use an on-line 24/7 enquiry service and take part in activities in support of local community.

According to the Office of National Statistics, in February 2005, 78 per cent of over 65 year olds had never used the Internet, compared to 35 per cent of society overall. One of the Digital Strategies seeks to improve accessibility for the digitally excluded and ease of use for the disabled and the Government is discussing with Help the Aged and others how best to address this issue.

People's Network in public libraries is a potent tool for delivery of lifelong learning, developing citizens' competence and confidence in using new technology. Library services, in association with other agencies, offer ICT training, from basic familiarisation to advanced, accredited training. 105,600 IT training sessions in 2003–04 and mediated access delivered opportunity for library users to enrich their quality of life and acquire new skills.

Assistive Technology

9.25. The Department of Health and the Office of the Deputy Prime Minister should make funds available to local authorities to set up the infrastructure needed for third generation social alarms. Local authorities should work closely with industry and with charities concerned with assistive technology in carrying this work forward.

The Government announced in July 2004 its plans to invest £80 million, over two years from April 2006, through a Preventative Technologies Grant. The purpose of the grant is to initiate a change in the design and delivery of health, social care and housing services and prevention strategies to enhance and maintain the well-being and independence of individuals. The Department of Health policy and implementation guidance makes it clear that the £80 million can be used to support all types of telecare, from first to third generation systems, and telehealth systems.

While the Office of Deputy Prime Minister makes no specific funding available to local authorities for alarm system expenditure, there are a number of funding sources, including the Supporting People grant programme, which authorities can use to invest in alarms if they wish. Any such additional investment would sit alongside, and support, the specific funding made available through the Preventative Technology Grant.

The Government recognises that before advantage can be taken of telecare, councils will need to ensure that the necessary infrastructure is in place. The Grant is intended to pump prime the process of infrastructure development and changes in the delivery of mainstream services.

9.26. The Department of Health's investment in assistive technology should be extended to include technologies and devices that can assist in monitoring health conditions and detecting early signs of health problems by individuals in the home.

The Preventative Technologies Grant is part of the Government's commitment to modernising and transforming care services provided by local authorities and the NHS and is designed to help local authorities and their partners address the challenges of a changing and ageing society. The Government expects councils to use the grant to invest in telecare to help support individuals in the community and help an additional 160,000 older people to live at home with safety and security and reduce the number of avoidable admissions to residential care and hospital.

The Department of Health policy guidance on developing telecare services and on the use of the Preventative Technology Grant (*Building Telecare in England*) requires local authorities to work in partnership with health, housing, industry and the voluntary sector when developing and delivering telecare services. It also makes it clear that the grant may be used to invest in technologies and devices that can assist in monitoring health conditions and detecting early signs of health problems in the home.

The Department of Health is currently undertaking a strategic review of assistive technologies. The outcome of that review will help inform any future bids, through the next comprehensive spending review, to extend investment in assistive technology and telecare. The Department will also work with economists, industry and academia to ensure that a robust evidence base, demonstrating the cost-effectiveness and benefits of these systems, is available to feed into the comprehensive spending review.

Industry and Commerce: the Missed Opportunity

9.27. The Government's policy of encouraging older people to remain in their homes as long as possible will be thwarted if industry does not respond to this challenge.

9.28. The Government should consult with the Design Council, the Confederation of British Industry, the Institute of Directors, the Federation of Small Businesses, the British Chambers of Commerce, trade associations and trades unions on how they can best play an active part in developing these markets.

9.29. Like the Foresight Ageing Population Panel, we encourage manufacturers and the finance and services sectors to seize this opportunity simultaneously to benefit their older customers and their shareholders.

A significant amount of activity is underway to ensure accessibility of information technology to all, including the elderly. More generally, whilst it is not the Government's role to advise business on what products and services to provide, it will write to the key organisations mentioned in paragraph 9.28 of the Committee's report, highlighting the Committee's recommendations.

The National Service Framework

9.30. The Department of Health must set out clear and measurable standards for assessing the health of older people, with particular emphasis on the care and treatment of those diseases prevalent in old age. Claims that those standards have been met should not be made unless they are supported by hard evidence.

The Government's National Service Framework for Older People (NSF) sets national standards and targets for the NHS and local authorities with social services responsibilities. In line with Shifting the Balance of Power (2003), the Government has reduced the number of NSF milestones classified as "must do" targets so that only the most crucial remain in this category. They are:

— developing specialist stroke services (by April 2004);

— better mental health services for older people (by April 2004);

— joined up falls prevention and treatment services (by April 2005); and

— capacity targets on intermediate care beds.

The independent health and social care inspectorates assess health and social care organisations against these measurable targets. They do so by a process of objective, rigorous and evidence-based assessment and this year have carried out a number of joint inspections across the health and social care system.

The Government has funded a major programme of research to evaluate the implementation and impact of the Older People's National Standards framework (NSF). This will provide a broad evaluation of the individual and combined impact of many of the service standards set out in the Framework.

9.31. We welcome the appointment of a "Government champion of older people". We believe that this must be a single minister of Cabinet rank who, whatever his or her title and departmental responsibilities, has full responsibility for bringing together and implementing all aspects of government policy relating to older people.

The Government welcomes this recommendation. The Department for Work and Pensions has the lead across Government on older people and David Blunkett, the Secretary of State will Chair the new Cabinet sub-Committee, Domestic Affairs Ageing policy, DA(AP). DA(AP) will oversee the Government's overall strategy on ageing as set out in its White Paper, Opportunity Age (March 2005, CM 6466i).

Cost Effectiveness

9.32. The initiation of studies of the cost-effectiveness of spending resources on prevention rather than treatment must be an important consideration for the Minister with overall responsibility for coordinating policy relating to older people.

The Government agrees with this recommendation. Specifically, the Department of Health's Vision for Adult Social Care sets out the need for strategic commissioning between local authorities, their health, voluntary, community and independent sector partners to support investment in preventative approaches to care for adults, which promote health well-being and independence. The Vision reinforces the key principles set out in the Department for Work and Pensions "Opportunity Age" strategy. It points to work that is already underway to build a credible evidence base to support preventative approaches to care for older people.

The Department of Health's Partnership's for Older People Projects (POPP) initiative is making available £60 million ring-fenced funding (£20 million in 2006–07 and £40 million in 2007–08) to council-led partnerships to establish and test local incentives, which will create a sustainable shift across the whole system towards cost-effective prevention for older people. The pilots, which will be operational from 1 May 2006 will test innovative approaches to doing this and will be subject to comprehensive evaluation at a local and national level. The Department of Health is working with key government departments to ensure synergy between the POPP programme and related policies focusing on the care of older people. The Government will ensure that lessons learnt are shared in a timely manner so that they can be fed into policy development across Government.

9.33. There must be effective supervision to ensure that it is the overall cost to the taxpayer which is considered, and not the cost to the budget of an individual department, to the NHS or to local government.

The Government agrees that in assessing policy proposals, the overall cost to the taxpayer should be taken into account. The Cabinet Office Better Regulation Executive provides guidance to departments to help them conduct regulatory impact assessments. In addition, HM Treasury produces investment appraisal guidance designed to promote efficient policy development and resource allocation across Government, emphasising the need to take account of the wider social costs and benefits of proposals, and the need to ensure the proper use of public resources.

Clinical Records

9.34. The Department of Health and the NHS should consult with the scientific community as to how the data generated by the NHS could be improved, the regulatory framework simplified, and the bureaucracy reduced.

The Government is aware that the quality of data in NHS systems could be improved and, together with the Audit Commission and the Healthcare Commission, has been involved in various initiatives to raise awareness and to encourage remedial action. In the next few years NHS organisations in England will be recording information on new systems that will link information together as part of the NHS Care Records Service. A component of this, the Secondary Uses Service will seek to address the problem of separated data collection by taking information directly from clinical systems and databases to provide a single comprehensive, consistent and high quality source of information for secondary purposes.

Following the Review of Arm's Length Bodies in 2004, the Government has also established the Health and Social Care Information Centre Special Health Authority. This aims to reduce the burden on frontline staff by streamlining data collections, and to improve public services by making NHS and adult social care information more accessible.

Clinical Trials

9.35. The Department of Health and the research councils should take steps to ensure that older people are not routinely excluded from clinical trials, and that positive steps are taken to include them in the testing of medicines to be used to treat conditions prevalent among older people. The Medicines and Healthcare Products Regulatory Agency should ensure that the pharmaceutical industry does likewise.

The Government shares the Committee's view on the importance of the appropriate inclusion of older people in clinical trials.

For research projects undertaken in the NHS, the inclusion and exclusion criteria for individual studies, including age limits, are scrutinised by various bodies. Research funders such as the MRC require that upper (and lower) age limits for participants in clinical trials are fully justified on scientific grounds, and that there should generally be no upper age limit on recruitment. NHS Research Ethics Committees must be similarly reassured about the characteristics of the research population, including age. The DH Research Governance Framework advises that, where relevant, account should be taken of factors such as age, sex and ethnicity in the design, undertaking and reporting of research. The newly formed UK Clinical Research Network (UKCRN) plans to record the age of all patients entered into UKCRN trials.

The Medicines and Healthcare products Regulatory Agency (MHRA) ensures that the pharmaceutical industry includes appropriate numbers of elderly patients in clinical trials. European guidelines recognise that the use of drugs in the elderly requires special consideration due to the frequent occurrence of underlying diseases, concomitant drug therapy and the consequent risk of drug interaction. They define elderly patients as over 65 years whilst recognising the importance of including those of 75 and above in clinical trials. They provide guidance on the disease categories, types of trials and an indication of numbers. The MHRA uses this guidance, as well as disease specific guidelines, as a basis for assessment of the adequacy of the data to support a marketing authorisation for a medicine for elderly people.

Longitudinal Studies

9.36. The Government should make additional funding available through the Department of Health and the research councils to implement joined-up programmes of longitudinal research on scientific aspects of ageing.

Funding for programmes such as longitudinal research on scientific aspects of ageing is provided both through the Science Budget and the Department of Health. The Science Budget is fully allocated until 2007–08. The review planned by the Funders Forum will provide valuable information to help inform the Research Councils as they prepare for the 2007 Spending Review.

The Department of Health commitment to longitudinal research on ageing is demonstrated in particular, by its ongoing funding of the English Longitudinal Study of Ageing (ELSA) jointly with the American National Institute of Aging. A number of government departments contribute to the funding of ELSA; ONS is responsible for its co-ordination. In addition to any new collaboration with partner bodies, it is keen to ensure that the insights from this rich national resource are fully exploited. Both the ESRC and the MRC fund significant datasets that impact on ageing research, encompassing both social and health-related aspects.

Two key groups have recently been formed to provide strategic direction to longitudinal work. The UK Data Forum aims to support a coherent and robust national data infrastructure for UK social and economic research. With representatives of all key social data set funders including Research Councils and Government Departments, the Forum will discharge its role through the development of a National Strategy for the Social Sciences.

The Health-Related Longitudinal Studies Oversight Group includes the ESRC, the MRC, the four Health Departments, the Wellcome Trust, and the Office of National Statistics. This aims to provide an opportunity for multiple agencies to take strategic oversight of health-related longitudinal studies and provide a co-ordinated approach to their development, management and funding. This will include longitudinal programmes that are specifically focussed on ageing, and those for which ageing is a secondary but nevertheless important feature.

Researchers

9.37. Multidisciplinary and translational clinical research, which is particularly important for ageing, has been hampered by the Universities Research Assessment Exercise. The Higher Education Funding Councils should, as a matter of urgency, consider how this problem can best be addressed in the forthcoming Research Assessment Exercise.

The Funding Councils are sensitive to this issue and are taking steps to ensure that concerns raised in the recent review of the Research Assessment Exercise (RAE) about the assessment of interdisciplinary and applied research are addressed in the 2008 RAE. For example, the guidelines they published for consultation earlier this year suggest that sub-panels may engage the expertise of specialist advisers particularly in the assessment of inter-disciplinary research. The particular issues in relation to clinical subjects have also been the subject of discussion between the British Medical Association (BMA) and the Chair of the RAE assessment panel for clinical subjects. The consultation on proposed assessment criteria for 2008 closed in September 2005 and the Funding Councils will now consider the points that have been made, before issuing finalised criteria.

Funding of Research: the Research Councils

9.38. We recommend that the Economic and Social Research Council should urgently and significantly increase the proportion of its funding available for ageing-related research. The Director-General of Research Councils should supervise this.

The ESRC views ageing as a priority area and this is demonstrated through its past and current investments and future plans described below. A significant example is through its commitment of significant funds to the new NDA Programme which ESRC has the administrative lead. ESRC has committed £5.4 million (pre-FEC) to the NDA. As this is future spend, it is not accounted for in the portfolio analysis.

Ageing research is a strategic priority for ESRC and is written clearly into its delivery plan. In addition to the NDA Programme, ESRC plan to do further work on the demographic changes that are occurring both nationally and internationally. This will include proposals for work on the changing dynamics of the family of which older people are a critical part.

ESRC has recently completed the commissioning of an initiative on Scottish Demography, funded in partnership with the Scottish Executive. ESRC are fully behind the NCRI's new Supportive and Palliative Care Initiative (SuPac), which obviously has major implications for older and elderly people, and is currently considering co-funding a proportion of the successful applications. The ESRC funded Centre for Microeconomic Analysis of Public Policy (CPP) located within the Institute of Fiscal Studies (IFS) has recently been awarded funding for a further five years. It undertakes research relevant to ageing on the labour force, savings, inequality and wealth. In addition, ESRC's responsive mode scheme continues to fund ageing research.

The longitudinal data-sets that ESRC fund are an invaluable resource in considering questions of ageing. The ESRC funds the National Child Development Study (NCDS) sometimes referred to as the 1958 cohort, the 1970 Birth Cohort Study and the Millennium Cohort study.

The ESRC portfolio analysis of ageing research quoted in table 6 of paragraph 8.23 and paragraph 8.28 of the report fell at a point between major ESRC programmes in the field of Ageing. The portfolio analysis supplied by ESRC was undertaken on grants live on 31 July 2002 and updated on 31 July 2004. Both dates exclude a significant amount of research funded through the Growing Older Programme. At least half of the projects within the programme had ended by July 2002 and all had ended by July 2004. The analysis did not include the longitudinal programmes referred to in the response to paragraph 9.36 above or the NDA Programme.

9.39. The research councils should ensure that when their scientific committees are considering applications for funding for ageing-related research, they include a majority of members with specific experience in these fields.

When considering applications made through the responsive mode, the research councils have to strike a balance in the membership of their peer review panels which must reflect the range of science under consideration, including ageing-related science. When the research councils implement initiatives that are focused on ageing research, the majority of the peer review panel membership will have expertise in age-related research. The best example of this is the forthcoming panel meetings to select the applications submitted to the NDA Programme. Great care has been taken in the selection of panel members to ensure there is appropriate representation to meet the needs of cross-disciplinary ageing research, and avoiding conflicts of interest. This is achieved by discussion between research council officers which takes place on a regular basis either informally or through the Cross Council Committee on Ageing Research (X-CAR).

Paragraph 8.32 of the report compares the composition of the review panels in the UK with those of the US National Institute on Aging (NIA). The NIA is responsible for a much more restricted portfolio of activities focused entirely on ageing than the UK Research Councils who have a much broader remit.

Funding of Research: the European Union

9.40. The Government must ensure that a very significant proportion of the resources allocated to the EU Seventh Framework Programme is set aside for ageing-related research. Members of the European Parliament should also press for this.

Although Government is not in a position to comment on the allocation of resources to age-related research under the seventh Framework Programme due to the continuing budget negotiations, it expects that this area of research will be well represented in the programme.

In the formal Commission's proposals for FP7, published in April 2005, the importance of age-related research has been addressed in a number of ways. Firstly, under the co-operation heading, it is stated that "health of the ageing population" will be addressed across activities within the Health theme. More specifically, under this theme "research on the brain and related diseases, human development and ageing" will be addressed under the "translating research for human health" activity.

The commission has also proposed to fund investigator driven research projects across all fields of research through the establishment of a European Research Council. This will provide an additional mechanism for funding basic research into areas including the possibility of age-related research.

In addition the research councils are currently in the early stages of investigating the possibility of developing a co-ordinated basic research programme on ageing through the existing UK co-ordinated ERA-NET programme on ageing (ERA-AGE). At a recent meeting of the ERA-AGE Forum, there was broad support for cross-European funding for ageing research using an extension of the ERA-NET mechanism available under Framework Programme 7. The Forum has now begun work to identify the priority areas for which support from the European Commission will be sought in 2006–07. The results of this could range from an extension of the current ERA-AGE programme, to include a cross-Europe call for grant applications in ageing using national funding budgets, to a more committed type of activity known as Article 169 which could bring significant additional funding for research from the European Commission.

Co-ordination of Research

9.41. Our conclusion is that the attempts at coordination so far made under the aegis of the research councils are woefully inadequate. The image we have is of a series of ill-thought-out initiatives which have long titles, short lives, vague terms of reference, little infrastructure, and no sense of purpose. A radical reorganisation is essential.

9.42. We conclude that the bodies currently responsible for the coordination of ageing-related research in the UK are not doing the job. The situation needs to be transformed. We believe however that this can be done without setting up a body modelled on the United States National Institute on Aging.

9.43. The responsibility for coordination must lie with the Department of Trade and Industry and the Office of Science and Technology. The Government's Chief Scientific Adviser will have an important part to play.

9.44. DTI and OST should set up a body with the membership, constitution, powers and funding necessary to provide the strategic oversight and direction of ageing-related research.

9.45. When deciding on the structure of this body, DTI and OST should learn from the successful structure of the National Cancer Research Institute.

9.46. Close collaboration with charities and private funders must be ensured by allowing them suitable representation.

9.47. There must be liaison with similar bodies in other countries, and developments in those countries must be taken into account.

9.48. Among the most important responsibilities of this body will be to promote research into ageing as a career for the best young researchers, and to supervise career development.

The Government agrees that there is a need to improve the level of co-ordination between Research Councils and between all funders of research into this area.

The issue of policy leadership on ageing is being addressed at the most strategic levels of Government. Late in 2004, the Government Chief Scientific Adviser's Committee (CSAC) consulted widely on "grand challenges" facing public policy where scientific research can play a major role in establishing the way forward. Three themes (including ageing) were agreed in March 2005 and Working Groups identified to develop those themes further. This is work in progress. With the support of other Chief Scientific Advisers, working across Departmental boundaries, it was agreed that the natural policy lead fell to the Department of Work and Pensions (DWP). DWP has the Ministerial Champion on Ageing and shares a major stake in the outcome with the Department of Health and others.

A wider exercise, across all analytical disciplines, was undertaken in Spring 2005 by the Coordination of Research and Analysis Group (CRAG) which also concluded that ageing was a priority for the whole of Government, to encompass all analytical and evidential disciplines.

In July 2005, Treasury announced a Comprehensive Spending Review (CSR) leading to a Spending Review 2007. Their announcement confirmed the impact of dependency ratios and ageing population as one of five Whitehall-wide policy priorities.

The Government is not convinced that a new body is needed to deliver the goal of improved research coordination. The Government believes that, where coordination between public sector and other funders is required that the Funders' Forum approach, where major stakeholders are brought together on an equal footing, is the most likely mechanism to achieve this result. The existing Funders' Forum on ageing brings together the relevant stakeholders and already carries out some of the functions highlighted in the Committee's Report and we should build on this rather than duplicating functions. The Government accepts that the Forum has yet to fully deliver its objectives, largely as a result of the precise way in which it has been set up. However improvements are already planned or underway and the Government has indicated its desire that these changes revitalise the Funders' Forum (FF).

The FF model has been applied successfully in other areas and its great strength is considered to be its ability to engage different stakeholders and to develop a common understanding between the stakeholders. The most successful of these to date has been National Cancer Research Institute (NCRI) which has evolved from the Cancer Research Funders' Forum but others funders' *fora* have also had their successes. Moreover, the Funders' Forum is now under the umbrella of the UK Clinical Research Collaboration (UKCRC), alongside other funders' *fora*. This will provide a more robust infrastructure for the Forum and enable close links with the UKCRC's clinical research networks on age-related disease, as well as its more general collaborative and coordinating activities. The secretariat of the FF will be located alongside the secretariat of other networks and funders carrying out similar roles, and will be able to draw on their knowledge and experience.

The FF has been revitalised in the following way:

— It has a new chairman whose sole focus is on ageing research (Chairman from the charity Help the Aged) and who is now planning the future strategy and operation of the FF.

— The new Chairman is currently undertaking a series of bilateral meetings with the members of the FF to ensure each organisation understands and agrees what is to be on the Agenda for the FF in the coming months. The next meeting of the Forum is due to take place on 24 February 2006.

— The foundations of a dedicated secretariat for the FF have already been laid with the research councils, health departments and some charities pledging a contribution towards a subscription to support the secretariat (as they do on a larger scale for NCRI).

— The FF is now also supported by the UK Clinical Research Collaboration alongside other funders' fora.

— The FF secretariat is expected to engage in an analysis of the research portfolios of all sponsors (such as that which was initiated by the research councils) using the same principles as the NCRI analysis in 2002. This should allow a co-ordinated approach to new national initiatives in ageing research, similar to those that have been enabled by the activities of NCRI.

—   Future developments in the FF will take place following further consultation with the stakeholders.

The FF will allow representatives from the charities and public sector to meet and exchange information about the research they sponsor and their future plans to tackle the emerging challenges in ageing research. The FF would be an ideal body through which liaison with other nations could take place to share best practice on the support and co-ordination of research, for example, with the US National Institute of Aging and especially other European nations since the UK currently co-ordinates the ERA-AGE programme supported under Framework Programme 6. Evidence available from other member states suggests that recruitment and retention of staff in the field of ageing research is a problem for a number of European nations: the FF offers an opportunity to initiate discussions across Europe on how to encourage and retain the best researchers to work in this field.

Development of secure career pathways for young researchers will be an important step in building research capacity in ageing research. The Department of Health, through the UK Clinical Research Collaboration, is already supporting a new initiative for developing academic careers in clinical research. This should provide an ideal framework for promoting ageing research more specifically. Partnerships across funding bodies will be essential to accommodate the broad multidisciplinary remit and interdisciplinary training needed to work at the interface between social, medical and basic science. Co-ordination between partners will also be required to plug gaps and avoid duplication of effort.

The RCUK would like to take this opportunity to give an update on the progress with the ESRC led cross council NDA programme. Subsequent to the evidence given by the councils, there have been two workshops attended by researchers from the scientific community. The workshops were planned and held to coincide with the call for Expressions of Interest (EoIs) for the major stream of funding under NDA known as Collaborative Research Projects. A total of 292 EoIs were received and approximately 360 potential applicants attended two workshops held in London during June 2005 to learn about the Programme and to meet researchers from other disciplines to develop collaborations. A total of 71 outline applications were received by the deadline of 29 July 2005. The workshops were the first opportunities in a long while to bring together researchers to discuss ageing-related research challenges in an holistic manner and the initial results suggest a high degree of excitement and enthusiasm for this Programme from the scientific community. The call for smaller (Programme) Grants will be made towards the end of this year.

RCUK would also like to clarify an issue raised in paragraph 8.55 of the Committees Report. The research councils are aware that there have been problems in the past with sponsorship of research grant applications that are relevant to more than one council. It is expected that the mechanisms currently in place and the increased awareness of the importance of cross-sponsor funding will solve these problems.

There is now a good track record of co-ordination between research councils covering a number of areas, ranging from co-funding of individual (cross-disciplinary) research projects to co-funding of entire research programmes. There are many examples of co-funding between the councils specifically in ageing research which are in addition to the cross-council programme *The New Dynamics of Ageing* and the *Innovative Health Technologies* Programme funded by ESRC and MRC. The co-funding of both research projects and programmes achieved by the councils in ageing research has been largely due to the activities of the Cross Council Committee on Ageing Research (X-CAR). For example, BBSRC and MRC have co-funded a grant from Professor Kirkwood made to MRC recently to study ageing in a population of 85 year olds in the UK while BBSRC and EPSRC have supported a major research grant from Professor Kirkwood on the systems biology of ageing. The origins of this grant can be traced to a grant co-funded by BBSRC and MRC in 2001.

The X-CAR has also enabled BBSRC and EPSRC to co-ordinate their support for a networking and pump-priming activity in cross-disciplinary ageing research through a grant to professors Lansley (Reading) and Faragher (Brighton). The initial round of pump-priming grants generated 85 applications involving cross-disciplinary research in ageing, highlighting the popularity of such a scheme.

November 2005

Memorandum by Professor Carol Brayne

9.3-9.5 The response appears to suggest that the current methods for monitoring disability free life expectancy and disease free life expectancy and quality of life are adequate by means of the systems listed. For some descriptors this is no doubt true, but such routine statistics capture the total population poorly (as institutional care is often not included and response rates can be low—eg ELSA's representation of the population, non institutionalised, is around 50 per cent) and do not capture conditions such as dementia at all well. No funding or plan exists in the UK to examine generational trends in dementia—the MRC CFA study (CFAS) investigators have now sought funding five times to carry out such work and been turned down each time. It is difficult to see what data could be captured in routine datasets to monitor trends and it is likely that dedicated studies will be needed for this kind of work for some time.

9.6 Very little of the physical activity response is geared towards the older population and the research base remains very embryonic for effective public health interventions—whether at community or individual levels. Interventions at the individual level seem likely to have health impacts at the population level within a manageable budget.

9.10 My impression is that the rhetoric of Choosing Health has been lost in the reorganization of the NHS and budgeting constraints.

9.11, 9.12, 9.17 From the front line researcher's point of view the sound bites here do not appear to be related to opportunity on the ground. It remains an inverted pyramid with many and constantly diverging committees talking to each other but not, in the end, making it any easier to generate high quality research output (the opposite at present unfortunately). It remains to be seen whether the aspirations of the new structures will work better.

9.32 These statements do not address the questions of evidence—lessons learnt are more about anecdotal experience of implementation—there does not appear to be a strategy for initiating research or rigorous evaluations to see whether spending £20–40 million on "council led partnerships" leads to any change in outcome. One example of policy implementation without research evidence is exercise referral schemes which now abound around the country but which are not based on sound trial evidence and become difficult to withdraw once in place.

9.16 This is sophistry. Because most people do die in old age, changes in the burden of health care and associated costs can best be predicted from demographic information. For conditions such as dementia and severe cognitive impairment age is the single most important variable.

9.34 Routine public health indicators and datasets do not include disability, sensory loss or dementia/cognitive status—mainly because these are so difficult to capture routinely. The response does not directly address the recommendation. The observatories in the UK are doing a good job of providing high quality data on all aspects of the population but they are potentially under threat with the current reorganization and have less speedy access to health service data than the commercial sector with fair higher quality governance arrangements. Disintegration of information systems and reduction of quality may well arise from the proposal that, for example, chronic condition care management be monitored through private companies (does this involve personal NHS data being handled by commercial companies owned outside the UK subject to US legislation?).

Since providing evidence to the Select Committee we have been attempting to set up re-interviewing of part of our research sample. Ethical approval is in place and we have experienced interviewers in each of the multi-centre locations ready to go. We are unable to start because the process of R&D approval, sponsorship and now CRB checks is taking, so far, seven months and each time we think we are ready to go there is another bureaucratic hurdle.

January 2006

Memorandum by the British Council for Ageing

EXECUTIVE SUMMARY

— Without firm political direction from Government the problems identified in the House of Lords report cannot be readily solved.

— The BCA urges the Government to explicitly prioritise funding for ageing research. It hopes that the next comprehensive spending review in 2007 will greatly enhance resources available to the community.

— The BCA suggest that the funding data and key recommendations of the House of Lords report with respect to the funding of ageing research are made available to those involved in the CSR.

— There should be a commitment to invest up to £5 million per annum in biological gerontology alone with appropriate levels of resource for clinical and social aspects of ageing.

— The BCA urges the Government to ensure that the research council funding panels call on the services of scientists and practitioners with a knowledge of ageing research and ageing issues.

— The BCA suggests that a large scale doctoral training programme be established in ageing research to increase the number of PhD students trained in this field.

PREFACE

The British Council for Ageing (BCA) represents the three learned societies with an interest in ageing issues, namely the British Society of Gerontology, The British Geriatrics Society and the British Society for Research on Ageing. This common committee was set up as a direct result of the suggestion made by their Lordships that a single and readily identifiable point of contact for policy makers would be helpful. Consequently, the chairs of the three learned societies felt it appropriate that comments to the House of Lords should be made via the BCA.

COMMENTS

We thank their Lordships for this opportunity to comment on the Government reply to *Ageing: Scientific Aspects*. The BCA endorses the Governments' conclusion that the major recommendations of the report relate to the need for additional funding of ageing research and the need for that research to be effectively co-ordinated.[10] The BCA would also add that the lack of training in the biology, clinical and social gerontology identified by their Lordships is an area of great concern.[11] Although the Government recognises that "progress has been made on all these fronts but that there is more that can be done"[12] it does not go on to outline anything concrete that it actually proposes to do. This is disappointing because the BCA believes that without firm political direction from Government (as was previously provided for ageing research through Technology Foresight)[13] the problems identified with research funding, co-ordination and investigator training are structural deficits that will prove extremely difficult to remedy.

Regarding the detail of the Government reply we offer the following suggestions:

Funding of Research: The statement that ". . . the government already invests heavily into research on ageing: including the scientific aspects"[14] seems at odds with the conclusions of the House of Lords inquiry. "Most of the research on ageing and health in the UK is focussed on specific diseases and medical conditions for which ageing is the single largest risk factor. However, there is little research on underpinning mechanisms of such diseases which may be linked to basic processes of ageing".[15] Our own analysis of investment by the UK in the biology of ageing indicates that the US spends four times our *per capita* budget in this area and has done so for decades. We estimate that Government needs to invest £5 million per annum in basic biology of ageing alone to maintain a significant research presence.[16] Whilst investment in ageing research may be significant in absolute terms it is not over generous relative to need and to the potential benefits which that research could yield.

The comment with regard to research funding priorities is somewhat disingenuous.[17] Since the inception of the Technology Foresight process, Government has undertaken the explicit prioritisation of some research areas relative to others. We do not argue for research into ageing which ignores other points in the life cycle. Rather we argue that a proper level of investment be made into an area which Government itself (through Foresight and EQUAL) recognises as critical for national quality of life.

Addressing the challenges of the ageing population will require major investment in longitudinal and related forms of research but will give major benefits in terms of designing more effective forms of intervention to combat the various chronic conditions affecting older people. Currently resources are spent on medical treatment to meet targets, when it could be more cost effective to spend money on prevention. This takes place against a background in which animal data clearly indicates that alteration to the rate of ageing can compress morbidity and lengthen productive life [Merry BJ and Holehan AM Effects of diet on aging. (1994) pp 147–170, in PS Timiras (Ed) Physiological basis of aging and geriatrics 2nd Edition CRC Press Boca Raton FL]. The best available human epidemiology also shows that compression of morbidity is occurring [Lubitz J, *et al* (2003). Health, life expectancy, and health care spending among the elderly. N Engl J Med, 349, 11, 1048–1055].

---

[10] Ageing: Scientific Aspects conclusions 9.11, 9.12, 9.17, 9.36, 9.41, 9.42, 9.43, 9.48. Reply by Government page 1, point 1.

[11] Ageing: Scientific Aspects conclusion 9.48.

[12] Reply by Government page 1, point 3.

[13] Technology Foresight panel on health and life sciences progress through partnership pp 20–22 (HMSO, 1995). Foresight joint task force on older people pp14-15 DTI/Pub5096/2-SK/09/00NP. URN00/1036.

[14] Reply by Government page 1, point 4.

[15] Ageing: Scientific Aspects conclusion 9–12.

[16] BSRA, written evidence to HoL Ageing: Scientific Aspects.

[17] Reply by Government page 1, point 4.

The lack of enthusiasm for ageing research in the Government's reply is particularly disappointing given the past record of at least some research councils. The BBSRC has conducted two very successful special initiatives (Science of Ageing and Experimental Research on Ageing) which produced many exciting breakthroughs some of which could be rapidly translated into clinical practice with proper funding. Similarly the EPSRC EQUAL programme has produced a raft of benefits for practitioners and older people in the area of design and the built environment. The BCA commends BBSRC and EPSRC for this effort. However, the House of Lords inquiry concluded that comparatively little was being invested by the MRC into ageing-related research and virtually nothing by the ESRC.[18] Although funding of the programme New Dynamics of Ageing represents a significant commitment for future spend by ESRC, the commitment of the MRC to ageing research appears to have improved little. We concur with this view and urge the Government to explicitly prioritise further funding for ageing research and hope that the next comprehensive spending review in 2007 will include a real financial commitment to all aspects of ageing research.

The continued involvement of life scientists and further development of a competitive UK science base in the field of ageing research will clearly depend upon the ability to gain funding. The Government state[19] "Government, research councils and others, are prepared to fund research, but delivery remains subject to worthwhile projects being proposed by competent researchers". The BCA does not disagree with this position, but would point out that this statement assumes that all worthwhile projects proposed by competent researchers are funded. This is sadly not the case and in a climate of restricted spending in which the research councils are unable to fund much of the high quality work that they receive, funding panels have to prioritise their spending. The research councils routinely operate to the highest standards of competency and professionalism, however if their panels do not include scientists with an understanding of the science of ageing we believe that they are less likely to prioritise applications in this area.[20] This is not because applications for support are judged unfairly but rather that a non specialist in any area finds it difficult to contextualise (and thus properly evaluate) novel research in an area which is not their own. This is a problem in all fields of science but is acute in ageing research because the size of the community remains small. Mechanisms to deal with this problem (eg Co-opting of extra panel members) already exist within the research councils so we argue for use of an existing instrument not the creation of a new process. The BCA would therefore urge the government to ensure that the research council funding panels include at least one member with a knowledge of ageing research and ageing issues.

Co-ordination of Research in to Ageing

The BCA welcomes the statement[21] that the OST will review spending on ageing research by the various funders and ensure coherence of funding in future spending reviews. It is not clear if this will be done in time for the 2007 Spending Review and also why the information supplied to the House of Lords inquiry could not actually be used to inform the 2007 review. If the review of funding of ageing research by the OST will not be done in time to inform the 2007 Spending Review, the BCA suggest that the funding data and key recommendations of the House of Lords report with respect to the funding of ageing research are made available to those involved in the CSR.

Taking in to account the above statement regarding the OST it is surprising that the government has decided not to base policy leadership and improved co-ordination of ageing research within either the DTI or OST as recommended by the inquiry.[22] This would appear to be a sound suggestion that might ensure that recommendations, for example those made by the Spending Review, convert to policies in the areas of funding of research, health and social policy relating to older people and to the arena of clinical training. Crucially, future co-ordination of research can only be useful if there is enough research to co-ordinate. Without strong, focused programmes of ageing research in the core remits of the research councils co-ordination, by whatever mechanism, is not especially useful. Assuming a suitable level of resource we favour a structure of ageing research programmes within the core remits of each council. The co-ordination of research council activity could then be co-ordinated by the existing cross council committee on ageing research (x-CAR), reporting directly to the DTI or OST. Interdisciplinary initiatives, such as the SPARC initiative which cover the "grey areas" between each council's core remit, are much more likely to be developed if this structure is in place and functioning. Translational research would also be greatly facilitated by such a structure if the DoH was also involved. BCA considers the appointment of a BBSRC representative (Dr Colin Miles) as the Chair of XCAR

---

[18] HoL conclusion 9–38.
[19] Reply by Government page 1, point 5.
[20] Ageing: Scientific Aspects sections 8.30, 8.31.
[21] Reply by Government page 11, point 61.
[22] Ageing: Scientific Aspects conclusion 9.43.

to be a very positive development. The BBSRC has an outstanding history of commitment to ageing research and Dr Miles enjoys the confidence of many biological gerontologists.

For the co-ordination of funding across research councils and other funders such as charities, the government has delegated responsibility to the Funders Forum.[23] While this grouping may improve upon delivery in this area under the capable chairmanship of someone dedicated to Ageing Research (Michael Lake), it is hard to see that the FF will have sufficient political bite unless it is reporting to, and has the backing of, a government department. In addition, whilst we welcome the spirit of the statement that the Funders Forum will be undertaking a portfolio analysis to identify priorities for future funding[24] and that the House of Lords recommendations will be taken in to account, this would appear to duplicate both the effort made by the House of Lords inquiry and the review that is proposed for the OST.

Training of young researchers in Ageing

It is important that there are sufficient competent researchers in the UK to design and execute international quality research on ageing issues. The government quite rightly point out that the BBSRC and EPSRC have funded an initiative, *SPARC*, aimed at increasing the number of researchers study in ageing. SPARC is a small initiative (£1.4 million over three years) but it has made a very good start. The standard of funding requests submitted by newcomers to ageing in the first call (June 2005) was so high that BBSRC and EPSRC have allocated additional funds to the second and final SPARC call (March 2006). Whilst this illustrates both the will of the community to work on ageing and the capacity to do so an "entry level" grants scheme cannot substitute for the provision of sustained funding. If ageing is not identified as a funding priority then new researchers will not become involved in ageing research and the existing body of researchers working in this area will decline. If the Government truly wants to see international quality ageing research carried out in the UK then they must ensure that there are sufficient scientists being trained in this subject area and that more existing researchers are attracted into the field. The BCA suggests that a large scale doctoral training programme be established in ageing research to increase the number of PhD students trained in this field.

The government accepts that capacity building in ageing research will rely upon secure career pathways for young researchers.[25] They inform us that the DoH working with the UK CRC is co-ordinating an initiative to develop academic careers in clinical research. There is no confirmation that gerontology will be highlighted in this initiative. It is also not helpful to merely state that co-ordination is required across funding bodies to achieve the multi-disciplinary training of young scientists in ageing. The BCA asks the government to outline what measures they are actually going to take to ensure that such training occurs.

In addition to the areas commented upon above the BCA was also disappointed with the governments response to issues concerning transport.[26] We think this section rather misses the point that there are major problems in the provision of transport in both urban and rural areas. Cities often present significant restrictions on the mobility of older people, especially those with a disability. For those who "age in place" in inner city communities, problems may be compounded by the decline of facilities essential to maintaining the quality of life in old age. Reductions in public transport have also presented a significant challenge to those living in rural areas. Major investments will be required to reduce problems of isolation and inactivity that result from these difficulties.

February 2006

Letter from Professor Peter Fentem, Chairman of the Research Committees of the Stroke Association

The evidence which I gave, and to which paragraph 9.13 refers, has been reinforced by the report from the National Audit Office Reducing Brain Damage: Faster Access to better stroke care (16 November 2005). This report together with the work of the Department of Health's Vascular Programme offers a good prospect that the implementation challenges for the NHS may be met.

The Government responses to the points made in paragraphs 9.16 and 9.17 are generally disappointing. So far as stroke is concerned the NAO report and more specifically the economic analysis which accompanied the report entitled Economic Burden of stroke in England emphasise the importance of addressing the burden of disability and its more effective management in the community.

January 2006

---

[23] Reply by Government page 24, point 127.
[24] Reply by Government page 24, point 129.
[25] Reply by Government page 25, point 131.
[26] Reply by Government page 13, points 69–72.

Memorandum by Help the Aged

EXECUTIVE SUMMARY

Help the Aged appreciates the lengths to which the Government has gone in responding to the Report of the House of Lords Select Committee. In this submission we have commented in some detail on the majority of the issues raised in the Government's reply but our major points of emphasis would be as follows.

— Much of the Government's response is defensive and backward looking. A clear opportunity to provide a visionary response which identifies research on ageing as a national priority is in danger of being lost.

— To an extent, there has been a disappointing failure either to identify or understand the evidence and some of its statements cannot be substantiated.

— The Government has not identified its willingness to initiate the "step-change" in funding necessary to secure adequate national capacity in research on ageing, without which the interests, health and well-being of the older population is at risk. Not only so but this reluctance to ring-fence new and additional money may be counter-productive in terms of the preventative savings which may accrue as a result and of the increases in GDP which arise as a consequence of investments in research and development. This position is at variance with the Government's ostensible commitment to delivering world class science and innovation.

— Similarly, the Government has failed to grasp the opportunity to take responsibility for the necessary co-ordination of research on ageing, which the Committee rightly stated needs to be transformed. Rather the Government is content to over-emphasise the role of the Funders Forum, a non-governmental alliance. Though the Forum is centrally placed to influence co-ordination of research, it is not in a position to direct it and carries neither the weight nor resources which are necessary to bring about fundamental change.

Therefore help the Aged calls upon the Government for:

— a clear statement making research on ageing a greater national priority.

— a "step-change" in funding levels for ageing research in the UK on a *per capita* scale of that of the USA. The current low order, inconsistent budget for research on ageing poses a real threat to the well being of older people. A stable, long-term regime of generous government funding must provide the basic research infrastructure to which charitable funding can contribute. The Comprehensive Spending Review for 2007 presents an ideal opportunity to meet this demonstrable need.

— the appointment of a "champion for ageing research" in a central government department, such as the Office of Science and Technology or the Department of Work and Pensions, to lead and direct a national research agenda on ageing. Such an appointment would be indispensable in the co-ordination of initiatives such as the Age Observatory, the New Dynamics of Ageing and the re-vitalised Funders Forum

DEMOGRAPHIC CHANGE

9.3—9.5

1. It is clear that the Government is considering the issue of demographic ageing at a high strategic level and that it is one of the "Grand Challenges" identified as a key driver of Government policy by CSAC and CRAG. The response demonstrates that the Government is seeking to inform its policies by bringing together data from a range of sources of information. However it is not entirely clear how the Government is integrating the lessons from its various departmental analyses into policy and practice. The proposed Observatory on Ageing (promised in Opportunity Age—the Government's strategy for ageing) could play a key role in this regard and it is surprising that the Government has not chosen to discuss this issue in more detail (or even identify its importance). Help the Aged has submitted evidence to the recent DWP consultation on the Observatory with the caveat that data collection and information sharing should be a fully integrated component of strategic research planning.

PROMOTING GOOD HEALTH: PHYSICAL ACTIVITY

9.6

2. The Government's response in this area is disappointing in that it ignores the wider agenda around physical activity at low levels and focuses only on sport. While sport is important, it is only one part of the broad spectrum of physical activity. The health benefits of physical activity in older age are well documented (eg the impact on falls) and should be given greater recognition.

3. There is little in the Government's response that is specific to older people, and nothing about how the barriers to participation in activity can be broken down. We were similarly disappointed that there was no recognition of the contribution of the National Coalition for Active Ageing nor any indication of how the Government would offer to support the Coalition's further development.

4. The Government refers to the new measures within the CPA which should help drive up access to sport and physical activity. We would like to see the assessment going wider than this, and looking at the broad range of opportunities provided to older people to enable them to lead active healthy lives—including consideration of issues of public transport, design of leisure facilities etc.

9.7

5. The Government's responses on promoting exercise are disappointing in their failure to address how exercise can be promoted amongst those in mid-life and beyond, despite the well documented evidence of benefit.

6. However this response is unsurprising given the lack of attention paid to the need to improve opportunities for exercise and activity amongst older people, within the recent White Paper Choosing Health

NUTRITION

9.9

7. The Select Committee's Report recommends that the links between healthy eating and healthy ageing need to be better understood and communicated to the public.

While the Government responds that advice and communication is already undertaken through the Food Standards Agency, the FSA has only one small booklet on nutrition aimed at older people "Eating for Later Life", which gives only very general advice. The public are bombarded with information from the health food industry and from newspaper reports on the benefits of a myriad of supplements that are claimed to prevent or treat many diverse diseases associated with later life and more research and focussed information should be made more widely available to older people. For example, the implementation of Vitamin D supplementation for older people living in institutions or house-bound, cognisant of the increased risk of bone fractures.

8. Since many older people do not have access to the internet, and are not used to this form of communication, it is not appropriate to use this mode of communication to older people.

9. While there has been high profile consideration of school meals and the diet of children, older people in both institutional settings or living independently have not been afforded the same attention. The Government should ensure that more appropriate research is undertaken by the FSA that places older people as a priority in determining the most effective modes of communication and behaviour change. The FSA should prioritise older people early in their studies such as the National Diet and Nutrition Survey. Strategic target setting for nutritional standards should prioritise older people in diverse settings.

10. The Government should ensure that there are extra resources so that the FSA do not have to divert existing funds for these purposes. It is vital that ring-fenced money is available for scientific research into the mechanisms by which nutrition affords better health in later life, through the research councils and the FSA. Without that, it is unlikely that sufficient funds would be available for the type of research required to take place.

11. *In summary, the Government's response in this area focuses primarily on the work of the Food Standards Agency (FSA). Clearly the FSA is making progress in some areas, however its specific advice for older people is inadequate, being limited to one booklet only. The response flags the "Eatwell" website, but given the low levels of internet access amongst older people, these messages will not necessarily reach older people. The public are bombarded with information from the health food industry and in the media on the benefits of a myriad of*

supplements that are claimed to prevent/treat many diverse diseases associated with later life. However often this is conflicting and can be confusing. More research and focussed information should be more widely available and targeted at the older segment of the population.

INDIVIDUALITY OF THE AGEING PROCESS

9.11 and 9.12

12. The Government emphasises the current work that is going on in relation to the UK with respect to biomarkers. We would recommend that international initiatives should be considered, such as the Biomarker Project in the USA which is under the aegis of the Alliance on Ageing Research and involves leading scientists from the NiA, the FDA and major pharmaceutical companies. We would criticise the Government's reply which appears not to appreciate the parlous funding position of research into the basic biology of ageing and its relationship to disease: there are only two major sources of funding in the UK, which are Research into Ageing and the BBSRC.

AGE-RELATED DISEASES

9.13 and 9.14

13. Stroke is an area of particular concern to Help the Aged and we have funded considerable research on the immediate treatment of cerebro-vascular events. Therefore we were pleased to note that the Select Committee Report calls for the Department of Health to make rapid treatment for stroke a priority.

14. Accordingly it was disappointing to note that the Government's response is to focus principally upon stroke services. The Government's response highlights the work that has been done to improve stroke treatment through the National Service Framework for Older People, but unfortunately progress against the framework has been somewhat disappointing. Stroke is still not given the priority that it deserves as one of the leading causes of morbidity and mortality among older people and there is a clear need for its priority to be elevated within the NHS. The Government's response ignores the point that little in the way of new treatments to limit the brain damage caused by stroke is available to patients, though there have been important research developments in this area. In particular, little action has yet been taken to improve the emergency response to stroke, which is so critical to minimising the impact of stroke on a person's quality of life. The need for the development of new effective treatments through research is particularly pertinent with an increasingly ageing population and the increase in the prevalence of stroke. In order to address this issue, research focused on the development of effective treatment must be prioritised alongside the availability of more stroke services.

AGE RELATED DISORDERS

9.15

15. While applauding the increase in dentistry training and the simplification of charging systems, access to NHS dentists is a widespread and well publicised problem. As oral and dental problems are a major concern in older people who are increasingly living with their own teeth intact, eg gingivitis associated with heart disease and problems with cleaning in people with arthritis of the hands, it is vital that more specialisation, research and access to dental services become available to older people, especially those in care homes or who have difficulty in mobility.

9.16 and 9.17

16. The House of Lords Report recommended more expenditure on diseases and sensory conditions associated with age. The Government's reply related only to question the relationship of age and the expenditure involved in meeting the costs of such conditions. The response was simplistic (in so far that it ignored the very considerable research data that are available on the complex economic relationships between ageing, healthcare and longevity) but was basically correct in identifying the real burden on health care costs as the increasing prevalence of long term chronic conditions (as evidenced by the Wanless Report for HM Treasury).

17. However, the lack of acknowledgement of the scale and burden of such conditions such as loss of vision, hearing, continence and mobility not only to those affected causing isolation and poor quality of life, but to society as a whole in terms of loss of income through earnings and active involvement in society is astonishing. Osteoporosis, to take but one example, is extremely common and clearly age-related; fractures arising from osteoporosis costing the UK around £5 million each day. It is of utmost importance to research effective treatments and preventative measures for osteoporosis which along with osteoarthritis very few people in the UK will escape suffering from in later life. This requires new funds, not redirected from other areas of medical research. The Government equally fails to acknowledge the costs which often fall to local authorities in providing social care support or in premature admission to institutional care.

18. In all these areas our view is that the Government's action has, unfortunately, been "too little too late" and its position on the relationship between ageing and health economics is demonstrably superficial.

THE BUILT ENVIRONMENT

9.18 and 9.19

19. In relation to the prevention of the very high excess winter mortality in the UK, the Government has failed to understand the research evidence in this area. Accordingly, it has concentrated its policy on the issues of indoor warmth and deaths from influenza. As long ago as 1997, the Eurowinter Study quite clearly showed that indoor and outdoor temperatures act independently in provoking excess winter deaths (EWD) from respiratory and thrombotic illness (heart attack and stroke). The data also clearly show that respiratory deaths, more dependent on indoor temperature, have in recent years been falling in number since the use of central heating has increased. By contrast, the number of deaths from arterial disease has not declined, since mortality in this instance is more related to exposure to external temperatures. Clearly, the Government has not recognised the contribution of so-called "high-risk" behaviour which appears to be a very important factor in explaining why Britain is so different to the remainder of Europe. There needs to be additional research on how health-related behaviour may be improved in the older population in the winter, with clear emphasis on understanding the risks of cold exposure, rather than on patronising advice. The Government's policies on improving the indoor home conditions of older people are to be welcomed, though the evidence appears to suggest that in themselves they will be insufficient to reduce the EWD figures to European levels.

20. Influenza, though of concern as a cause of death in the winter, plays a very small role in the overall EWD data except in epidemic years.

21. Since the Government made its response it has now made some significant progress in its work to reduce fuel poverty through the Warm Front programme—particularly by making available £300 per household to older households without central heating and otherwise ineligible for assistance. Similarly, the Warm Front Plus initiative is to be welcomed.

22. Clearly, however, action will continue to be needed to tackle fuel poverty (a significant risk factor in winter deaths)—particularly as the numbers of those in fuel poverty increase as fuel prices rise.

23. We continue to be in discussions with Government regarding the Lifetime Homes Standard (LHS) and have welcomed the announcement that the LHS will be built into the Code for Sustainable Homes. However, we are disappointed that the Standard hasn't been included in Part M of the Building Regulations. It is additionally disappointing that the ODPM appears not to have a discernable strategy for older people's housing.

TRANSPORT

9.20

24. We are still awaiting the results of the DVLA review, so are unable to offer further comments at this stage.

9.21 and 9.22

25. Help the Aged has welcomed the recent acknowledgement by Government, in the Social Exclusion Unit Report A Sure Start to Later Life, of the need to ensure older people's needs are considered in transport planning, and its recognition of the importance of flexibility in transport provision and in the availability of concessionary fares.

COMMUNICATION

9.23

26. We would commend the Government for its approach to Telecare, as a primary concept in the maintenance of independence of older people in their own homes. Help the Aged is represented on the R&D Commissioning Panel (DH) for research in this area. However, in our experience there has been a serious failure to recognise the importance of a fully engaged user-participation in the research proposals in this programme. Consequently, implementation of technology solutions are likely to be made difficult by the consumer resistance which is generated by the absence of a sense of ownership.

9.24

27. The Government focus on broadband access rather misses the point that it is internet access in general that remains the problem for older people. There remains a need for more action to address the digital divide and to make new technology accessible and attractive to older people. Help the Aged continues to work with the Government in order to resolve the marginalisation of older people in technology areas.

ASSISTIVE TECHNOLOGY

9.25 and 9.26

28. In our experience, there is considerable inconsistency in the way in which the Preventative Technology Grant is deployed. Though it is commendable that DH policy allows expenditure to support all kinds of telecare, the interpretation of this has been very wide and appears to have resulted in expenditure in some instances on non-telecare areas. Careful audit is required to ensure adherence to the policy objectives. We would also add that our experience is of a general inadequacy of commissioning skills in Primary Care Trusts. This is a critical level at which buying-in decisions are taken and our recent work with the Adam Smith Institute indicates poor skills in this area.

INDUSTRY AND COMMERCE

9.27–9.29

29. Help the Aged receives numerous requests from the private sector to enable greater penetration of the ageing sector of the population to products and services, for which there is little take-up at the present time. There are very many reasons for the marginalisation of older people, including accessibility, design, marketing, social psychology (fear of technology; technology awareness and acceptance) and economic factors. There is no "industry" benchmark for "ageing compliance" in testing or design and in the absence of such criteria marketing to the older population is arbitrary and difficult. It therefore behoves the Government to exercise much more leadership in creating partnerships to resolve these difficulties and in addition, there is a considerable shortfall in the volume of research funding in the area of ageing and design. New and additional research funding in this area would, in our view, be extremely valuable. The remit of the DTI to improve the levels of private sector R&D should be exercised considerably more in this area.

THE NATIONAL SERVICE FRAMEWORK

9.30 and 9.31

30. The Government's response to the Select Committee's challenge on measuring progress in older people's health is to highlight the National Service Framework (NSF). However, one of the biggest challenges facing the NSF is the fact that with the moves towards devolution in the NHS, the Department of Health simply does not have access to performance data at a local level. This means that the Department frequently does not know how the implementation of the NSF is actually progressing on the ground in any comprehensive way. The Healthcare Commission evaluation is due to be published very soon, and we expect that it will highlight the fact that progress in implementation of the NSF has been variable.

Cost Effectiveness

9.32 and 9.33

31. The Government's new interest in preventing avoidable decline is very welcome. Help the Aged is extremely supportive of the POPPs programme (para 100) and has been involved in its implementation. Furthermore, the Vision for Adult Social Care gave a welcome focus to the preventative message which is a central pillar of the White Paper "Our Health, Our Care, Our Say". The vast majority of patients with chronic, long-term conditions are themselves older people and we would further recommend that further consideration is given to how older people specifically can be supported to manage their own health.

32. However, the reality is that most local councils and the NHS simply do not have the resources to do anything more than respond to those with the most pressing and urgent needs. The access criteria for social care which were introduced by the Fair Access to Care Services guidance mean that most local authorities are only providing services to those with "critical" needs — leaving older people with lower level needs to find support from elsewhere. Since 1997, the number of older people receiving low level social care support has fallen by almost one third, as services are increasingly targeted at those with more complex needs.

Clinical Records

9.34

33. The Government's response rather seems to miss the point of the original recommendation and has therefore failed to offer any comment on whether and how the scientific community might be given better access to NHS data, to enable the use of that data to answer scientific questions.

Clinical Trials

9.35

34. Help the Aged has recently completed some work on the age and gender bias in clinical trials of interventions that will be ultimately used primarily on older people, which has shown that there remains clear under representation of older people, particularly women, in clinical trials resulting in under prescription of key drugs in clinical practice. It is unacceptable that a section of the population is excluded from evidence-based medical practice.

35. Legislative action particularly in US has tried to combat exclusion of older people and women from medical research. A recent study examined discrimination in clinical research in the last three decades to see if there are differences in publications between the UK and USA. Significant ageism still exists in clinical research both sides of Atlantic, although more progress appears to have been made in US in reducing sexism. This issue should be taken more seriously, and steps to ensure that it does not continue should be put in place through regulatory bodies, ethics committees, academics and industry.

Longitudinal Studies

9.36

36. Longitudinal studies are different from other more mechanistic short-term hypothesis-driven investigations in terms of size, cost and duration. It is therefore important that funding for these types of important studies is viewed differently from most research projects, and that ring-fenced funding is provided.

37. The Government emphasises its contribution to the funding of the English Longitudinal Study of Aging without identifying the much lower proportion of the costs that it is meeting in relation to funding from the USA. Nor does it identify that in Wave 1 and 2 of the study, it inadequately met the costs of data collection by some £600,000 and in Wave 3 it provided only £4.6 million of the £5.9 million requested. Furthermore, the Government does not identify that these costs are for data collection only and not for analysis, as in the case of the more medically driven studies such as the Whitehall 2 Study and the Baltimore Longitudinal Study. There are equally large data banks, such as the 1946, 1958, 1970 and Millennium Cohorts and ONS data which remain to be analysed further. There is little or no identifiable funding for these projects (less, possibly, the second (project) phase of the NDA) which could contribute significantly to the fundamental understanding of the inequalities of health across the life-course. Equally, there is little funding available for important international comparisons, particularly in Europe where the short-term nature of the Framework

Programmes discriminates severely against the possibility of successful longitudinal data collection. These considerations need to be taken into account more seriously by the Government than their response appears to indicate.

RESEARCHERS

9.37

38. Help the Aged welcomes the Government's attention to the issues raised with respect to the Research Assessment Exercise. We would simply re-inforce the apparent disparity which exists between the concept of Units of Assessment and the requirement for multi-disciplinary research, as exemplified by the New Dynamics of Ageing. The increased importance of the multi-disciplinary approach is a natural conceptual development which has arisen both from theoretical considerations and the perceived superiority of multi-disciplinary research in providing practically beneficial research solutions. This disparity presents a real difficulty for researchers who must cope with the tensions arising from the demands of the RAE on the one hand and the demands of the funding bodies on the other. This issue must be addressed by the Higher Education Funding Councils.

THE RESEARCH COUNCILS

9.38

39. Help the Aged has excellent working relationships with all the research councils, not least of all because of its role as current chair of the Funders Forum. To some extent, the Councils are placed in a difficult position because they are required to fund out of their vote and the volume of funding on ageing research is to a large extent determined by the response from the academic community. However, in our view both the recent response to the New Dynamics of Ageing and that of our recent Major Gifts Appeal reveals that the capacity for research on ageing is much greater than the volume that would be determined by the "ageing" allocation of the Councils budgets. In other words, demand exceeds supply. It is our position that the Government should make available new and additional funding, dedicated to ageing research. Without a "step-change" in funding availability, there will be damaging consequences for the UK research capacity on ageing, with consequent damage to the long-term interests and well-being of older people. The Comprehensive Spending Review provides an ideal opportunity for the Government to demonstrate the extent of its commitment to ageing research.

THE EUROPEAN UNION

9.40

40. In general, the Government's reply in this area completely lacks credibility and is grossly ill-informed. In particular, there is no evidence that ageing research will feature strongly in the next Framework Programme. The Programmes are politically and economically driven, that is, they are designed to provide research programmes to improve the economic position of the EU *vis-à-vis* the USA. Ageing will only feature in so far that it is subsumed into other categories, such as technology, medical and health-related research. This is confirmed in paragraph 120.

41. The issue of a European Research Council is virtually a "non-starter". Our understanding is that there is little political support for this in the EU and even less motivation to support it financially. Secondly, our experience of academic opinion in the European Forum is that it is equally divided both "for" and "against". The Government's apparent optimism for significant, real and lasting funding and strategic thinking from the EU on ageing research is seriously misplaced. At the present time, only developments via ERA-AGE are under consideration by the Research Councils. The level of funding from the EU, including ERA-AGE pales into insignificance in comparison to the USA and even the UK. Help the Aged has presented considerable evidence to this effect to the Select Committee.

CO-ORDINATION OF RESEARCH

9.41–9.48

42. In Help the Aged's submission of evidence, we identified two major issues which are critically important to the future of ageing science in the UK: one is the low-order, inconsistent level of expenditure on ageing research and the other is the absence of clear leadership in co-ordinating a national agenda on research. The two issues are inextricably linked since any "vision for ageing" can only be effectively translated into action with adequate funding. We would re-iterate the position that failure to address these issues adequately represents a real threat to the well-being of our increasingly older population. Not only so but this reluctance to ring-fence new and additional money may be counter-productive in terms of the preventative savings which may accrue as a result and of the increases in GDP which arise as a consequence of investments in research and development.

43. There was substantial, some would say acerbic, criticism in the Report on the issue of research co-ordination. In the face of the indisputable evidence produced in the Report, it is not surprising that the Government "agrees that there is a need to improve the level of co-ordination between Research Councils and between all funders of research into this area". In essence, the Government's answer to this criticism is to defend the existing provision and in particular to re-emphasise the role of the Funders Forum.

44. Help the Aged currently holds the chair of the Forum and together with the membership has embarked upon an ambitious, though realistic, series of initiatives designed to improve its co-ordinating role, to produce a compelling case for the improved prioritisation of ageing research and to influence the spending review in 2007. These initiatives are:

(a) A business meeting of the Forum on 24 Feb 2006 (the first since June 2003).

(b) A "Vision for Ageing" workshop sponsored by Unilever (on 21–23 May 2006 in The Hague) opened by Michael Lake CBE (Chair of the Funders Forum) and with the keynote address given by Lord Sutherland.

(c) A national conference (The Future of Ageing Research in the UK) on 1 November 2006 in London, in collaboration with the New Dynamics of Ageing.

45. Though we have every confidence that these initiatives will be successful and that they are eminently necessary, there are sound reasons why these and other activities of the Forum are insufficient in themselves to "transform" the co-ordination of research. These reasons are as follows.

(a) The Funders Forum itself does not have a dedicated research budget, other than the individual budgets of its members. It is not believed that it is the Government's intention to directly or indirectly fund the increase in the Forum's remit or portfolio of activities which would be necessary to achieve the Government's own aspirations for the Forum, particularly its the international role.

(b) The recommendations of the Forum are not binding on the funding or strategy   decisions of its members.

(c) The Forum has no formal nor direct relationship with any department of State.

(d) The Forum is unique in the widespread and eclectic nature of its members' interests, a feature which would mitigate against the development of an "ageing research institute" (as in the case of the NCRI) or research networks (as in the case of the UKCRC).

(e) With respect to the UKCRC, the interests of the Stroke Association and the British Heart Foundation are already subsumed within the UKCRC networks, each with a co-ordinating centre.

(f) The success of other Forums has been mixed; whereas the Cancer Funders Forum has achieved considerable co-ordinating progress, that of others has been much less certain.

46. It is our view that a much more coherent and integrated approach by Government is necessary to bring together the apparent disparate initiatives of the various departments, though it is recognised that something approaching this will emerge from the cross-departmental bid, led by the DWP, for the comprehensive spending review in 2007. In our evidence we called for a clear statement from Government making ageing research a national priority. There has been a lamentable failure to do this and rather than produce a visionary statement on the future of ageing research, the Government has resorted to a defensive and backward looking posture.

47. *In summary, we find the Government's position on research co-ordination to be untenable, lacking vision and without any clear and substantial plan for the future. Verbose arguments related to new initiatives such as the New Dynamics of Ageing (welcome though it is) only serve to illustrate the absence of a long-term, well funded and co-ordinated agenda for ageing research in the UK. Clear leadership is necessary to co-ordinate the ageing agenda*

of the various Government departments, including the positioning and role of the proposed Observatory on Age. The CSR 2007 represents an ideal opportunity for the Government to ring-fence new and additional funding to achieve the per capita levels of expenditure as in the USA. Our recommendation is for a "step-change" in funding levels for ageing research in the UK and for a clear departmental responsibility for a highly prioritised national agenda for ageing research.

January 2006

Memorandum by Professor Tom Kirkwood, Specialist Adviser to Sub-Committee I (Ageing: Scientific Aspects)

The content and tone of the Government response are intensely disappointing. My impression is that the report was read and responded to with exactly the same lack of engagement and understanding of the current challenges and opportunities that has produced the unsatisfactory position highlighted by the Committee. The clear impression is that population ageing is seen merely as a "problem", which must take its turn among others, rather than a fundamental change in the fabric of UK society which is overdue for special strategic attention.

Specific comments are as follows (paragraph numbers refer to those in the Government response):Para 4. It is questionable whether the adverb "heavily" accurately describes current investment. The issue of competing priorities is important but the competitions listed here arise more from misunderstanding of the key scientific issues than from fact. Each member of today's population is highly likely to make the entire journey from infancy to old age; there are scientific connections between birth, early years, childhood and adolescence that have major impacts on health and quality of life in middle and old age. These need much greater attention and this should be driven by the need to understand ageing. As for the balance between research on ageing itself and age-associated disease, the response appears to miss the significance of the Committee's arguments, based on evidence submitted, that understanding why aged cells and tissues are intrinsically more vulnerable to pathology may be the most direct route to developing novel interventions and therapies for age-associated conditions.

Para 5. The challenge, as indicated in the report, is to secure proper assessment of what is "worthwhile".

Para 6. It is disappointing that there is not more recognition of the interactions between biological, medical and psychosocial factors.

Para 21. While it is welcome that the importance of sport and physical activity is recognised and will be monitored, it would be good to know how effectively the Report's recommendations have been disseminated to local authorities, etc.

Para 49. It is true that the MRC (and also the BBSRC) has now taken up the issue of biomarkers. However, it is not clear that ageing has yet been identified as a specific priority in this area and there are distinctive issues about biomarkers in relation to underlying mechanisms of ageing.

Para 52. It is still not clear how seriously the Department of Health takes the need to build links with scientific aspects of ageing in developing their agenda. Much will depend on their engagement within the Funders Forum. Even with the planned reinvigoration of the Funders Forum, this may not be a structure with the power to effect the necessary change.

Paras 54 and 55. More needs to be done than merely focusing on cancers prevalent in older people. The scientific links between ageing and cancers also need to be addressed.

Para 58. It is not at all clear what the first sentence is intended to mean. See also comment on para 4, above.

Para 60. The Report argued for a step change which requires urgent action if it is to inform the Spending Review in 2007.

Para 73. This is very lame and suggests that the importance of the issue has not been recognised.

Para 79. This is highly questionable. One needs to ask what factors have been taken into account in assessing "economic efficiency" and equity. With the increasing tendency for key information and services to be made available via the internet, those with limited access to broadband are severely disadvantaged. Based, for example, on experience of difficulty in accessing broadband in rural communities within the North East, even after significant efforts by the RDA to promote development of the necessary infrastructure, it is clear that there is still significant exclusion.

Para 80. I am not sure that the EC views can serve as a useful comparator, other than defensively. What the Report highlighted was an opportunity that could be realised by the UK taking a lead.

Para 93. It would be interesting to know how the DoH strategic review of assistive technologies is being done. Does it have the necessary ingredients for vision?

Para 98. This goes against the specific recommendation in the Report without giving any reason why.

Paras 112–116. This is a rather unconvincing defence of ESRC investments. The only figure given is the £5.4 million committed to the NDA. As the Report noted, this initiative is not very big, when the sum is considered in relation to the scale of the issues to be addressed.

Paras 117–118. These do not address the issue raised in the Report, that peer review panels within each Research Council may lack the expertise to judge what is worthwhile. We are told only that the NDA panel is cross-disciplinary. This may be so but it misses the major point.

Para 112. The specific achievements of ERA-AGE are not indicated.

Memorandum by the Stroke Research Network

The National Audit Office report provides evidence to rebut the suggestion from the government (9.13 and para 53, 9.30 and para 95) that the current services are adequate. Although specialist stroke services are present in most Trusts, very few (< 5 in England and about 5 in Scotland) provide a 24 hour specialist hyperacute service that can deliver effective interventions such as thrombolysis. The problem is not location of scanners in A&E departments; it is access to C/T scanners wherever they are. The NAO report specifically mentions the very low scanning rate of patients in the first 24 hours. It would be logistically straightforward, clinically justifiable and financially cost-effective (HTA report by Wardlaw *et al*) to set a standard that all patients with suspected stroke should be scanned immediately on admission to hospital, ie to insist that scanners are used appropriately.

In research terms, it will be important to ensure future imaging investment, both service in NHS and research (eg the recent Wellcome infrastructure call), is integrated with stroke services and research groups: state of the art imaging facilities need to be developed on sites that see large numbers of stroke patients acutely.

9.3 Stroke related disability is probably the major cause of disability and loss of disability-free life expectancy in older people.

9.7 SRN supports research into establishing the benefits of exercise, nutrition and other life-style modifications in preventing stroke in older people and the development of effective strategies to achieve this in the older population.

9.17 The SRN supports development of research programs examining alleviation of long term disability related to stroke.

9.18 The SRN is discussing with the Met Office a study to determine the effect of changes in outdoor temperature and stroke incidence, which would have implications for development of programs to reduce the increased stroke incidence in older people that may occur during spells of cold weather.

9.33 Investment in acute stroke services has been neglected because the financial benefits of acute stroke units and treatments are accrued by community services but the costs fall on hospital Trusts (another point made by the NAO report).

9.34 A very important point. We consider the opportunities to improve research and access to patients and their anonymised data need to be considered in NHS data systems. For example we should be asking people routinely for permission to use anonymised data in research and to be able to use their details to approach them about research studies.

9.35 Important point in relation to stroke trials which I think we have mostly addressed in UK but not in some European trials (ECASS III, ESPRIT)

9.36 Translational research has not been adequately developed for stroke in UK and is hampered by lack of integration of MR/PET and other research imaging with well organised stroke services (both acute and rehabilitation). Animal researchers in the UK, whose work may be crucial for development of new treatments in stroke, are under intense pressure.

9.40 EU funding is very difficult to access particularly for clinical research.

January 2006

Memorandum by Professor Anthea Tinker and Ms Claudine McCreadie

1. We have no specific comments about the response relating to the main areas where we gave evidence ie assistive technology and ageing. As can be seen the Government are investing in this area of provision and research.

2. We are, however, not very impressed with the overall impression given by this document which is very complacent. For example the research mentioned at the end (including the New Dynamics of Ageing programme and the cross-disciplinary ageing grant (SPARC) to Lansley and Faragher) are very small compared with the research which is undertaken in other areas.

3. Similarly the message, which AT emphasises in oral evidence, that older people have strong views and can suggest solutions to problems, does not seem to have been taken on board. For example the use of the words "the elderly" in the latter part of the response does not inspire confidence. The tone is patronising. The emphasis should be on making better use of the talents of older people.

4. There is a need for a strong lead from Government on ageing issues. This document indicates that responses are uncoordinated. DWP are said to be the lead but this is very low profile. Opportunity Age is a good start but much more need to be done to publicise the messages in this document.

January 2006

RECENT REPORTS FROM THE HOUSE OF LORDS
SCIENCE AND TECHNOLOGY COMMITTEE

Information about the Science and Technology Committee is available on **www.parliament.uk/hlscience/**, which also provides access to the texts of Reports. General Parliamentary information is available on **www.parliament.uk**.

Printed in the United Kingdom by The Stationery Office Limited
3/2006   331732   19585